W0082651

PARADISE FOUND

PARADISE FOUND

Norman Manea & Hannes Stein

The Sheep Meadow Press

The Sheep Meadow Press
Rhinebeck, New York

Copyright (c) 2013 by Norman Manea

All rights reserved. No part of this publication may be reproduced or transmitted in any form or by any means, electronic or mechanical, including photocopy, recording, or any information storage and retrieval system, without permission in writing from the publisher, except in the case of brief quotations in reviews.

Designed and typeset by The Sheep Meadow Press Distributed by The University Press of New England

All inquiries and permission requests should be addressed to the publisher:

The Sheep Meadow Press
PO Box 84
Rhinebeck, NY 12572

Library of Congress Cataloging-in-Publication Data

Manea, Norman.
  [Gespräche im Exil. English]
  Paradise found / Norman Manea and Hannes Stein.
      pages cm.
  ISBN 978-1-937679-27-9
  1. Manea, Norman--Interviews. 2. Manea, Norman--Childhood and youth. 3. Novelists, Romanian--20th century--Interviews. 4. Holocaust, Jewish (1939-1945)--Romania--Personal narratives. I. Stein, Hannes. II. Title.
  PC840.23.A47Z46 2013b
  859'.334--dc23
  [B]
                        2013010774

Contents

An Introduction by Hannes Stein   vii

PART ONE: Disorder and Early Sorrow   11

PART TWO: The Moment of Liberation   15

THE THIRD DIALOGUE: On Happiness   19

THE FOURTH DIALOGUE: Comrade Stalin   23

THE FIFTH DIALOGUE: The Jewish Monopoly   32

THE SIXTH DIALOGUE: About Women   38

THE SEVENTH DIALOGUE: Without Glasses in the Camp   45

THE EIGHTH DIALOGUE: The Long Goodbye   49

THE NINTH DIALOGUE: On Israel   54

THE TENTH DIALOGUE: Pedestrian in America   59

The Eleventh Dialogue: The Rabbi   65

THE TWELFTH DIALOGUE: The Right to Stupidity   69

THE THIRTEENTH DIALOGUE: The Scandal   75

THE FOURTEENTH DIALOGUE: On Celan, Fondane, and Cioran   82

THE FIFTEENTH DIALOGUE: A Letter to No One   88

THE SIXTEENTH DIALOGUE: On Nabokov   95

THE SEVENTEENTH DIALOGUE: A Proust from the East   98

Addendum

A Conversation Between Norman Manea & Ilana Shmueli   101

Introduction to the Letters of Celan & Shmueli:
Needing and Being Needed   123

An Introduction
by Hannes Stein

In the winter of 2009 I climbed into a train at Manhattan's Penn Station headed toward the snow-covered Hudson valley eighty-five miles north for the Rhinecliff station, where I took a taxi to Bard College.

The Jewish-Romanian-American writer Norman Manea has been professor of literature there for more than twenty years. He lives in a house on the university campus in the periods when he isn't staying in his Manhattan apartment.

I first met Manea in 2005 when he was the guest of the American Academy in Berlin. At the time, I was one of the editors of the literary weekend section of "Die Welt," a German newspaper. I had already known his books for some time. His short story collections Robot Biography and Training for Paradise had been published by Steidl Verlag. The two books (unfortunately long out of print) impressed me chiefly for two reasons. One: As it happened, I had many friends who were part of the dissident scene in East Germany, as a result of which I had a pretty clear picture of life in the sordid communist police states. Norman's stories brought back many conversations I had had with people like my friend Juergen Fuchs (who spent nine months in a prison run by the Stasi, the East German secret police) or Wolf Biermann, the German Bob Dylan (who had been banned in the GDR for twelve years). Romania, as Norman Manea described it, thus was not a completely foreign country to me; I recognized the shabbiness, the absurdity, the pettiness of it all. Only Ceaucescu's Romania was much more Byzantine – and more corrupt – than the East German variety of totalitarianism. Two: Norman Manea is a survivor of the German genocide against the Jews. As it happens, I am Jewish myself. I grew up with stories of the holocaust; Norman Manea could be an uncle of mine. All of this sounds pretty gloomy, which gives a false impression. For the truth of the matter is that Manea – like Franz Kafka – can be rather funny, sometimes even lighthearted. This, too, spoke to me: his sense of humor, his laughter in the dark.

I vaguely remember a reading of his at the "Literaturhaus" in Hamburg, a patrician villa close to the Alster Lake at which highbrow cultural events took place. It must have been right after the fall of the Berlin Wall, or maybe slightly before. In any case, timidity kept me from approaching the writer then.

We both found ourselves in New York after I had won a greencard in the lottery and become "Die Welt's" cultural correspondent in the US. And once I had overcome my timidity, we reconnected. One day Norman Manea and I decided to set up a long interview. I collected my tape recorder and headed his way. We spent three days together at Bard College. We would begin discussion right after breakfast and return to work in the afternoon after a Romanian siesta. In one of the intervals, on a fine, misty, drizzling day I visited the grave of Hannah Arendt, buried on campus beside her husband, Heinrich Blücher. One difficulty proved insurmountable, however. Despite my efforts, the language of Eugène Ionesco and Mircea Eliade, Nicolae Ceașescu and Ion Luca Caragiale, Ion Antonescu and Emil Cioran remained a book of seven seals to me, so Manea and I spoke English, the language of all expatriates. Cella Manea, Norman's wife, cooked us divine meals and made sure our dialogue wouldn't get too far off track. I eventually gathered fifteen hours of recording.

This book presents the most significant passages of the interview: information about the life and work of a writer vital to modern literature.

Hannes Stein
August 2010
New York

–PART ONE–
Disorder and Early Sorrow

Hannes Stein: What is your first childhood memory?

Norman Manea: It's interesting, I have no clear memory of the period before deportation. I was five years old when I was deported in October 1941. My memory is hazy, so to speak. One image has remained with me, though: a sunny day in front of my grandfather's bookstore. The door to the shop is open. That's the image: a sunny day and an open door.

HS: That's from before the deportation?

NM: Yes. After the deportation my grandfather no longer existed, the bookstore no longer existed, many things no longer existed.

HS: It's a happy memory.

NM: I can't explain it. I don't really know the context. I know that I was a spoiled child—spoiled by my family and probably by my grandfather, whom I was very close to in the camp. He was a very special person, full of humor, wise. He died soon after our arrival in camp, during the first harsh winter.

HS: In Transnistria.

NM: Yes, and that encounter with death was the first great shock of my life. I didn't know what death meant, and the disappearance of my grandfather terrified me greatly.

HS: Do you still recall the deportation itself?

NM: I can call up images clearly, but with no clear chronology. Intense physical sensations are attached to those images: fear, hunger, cold, sickness. Yes, I have memories. I have a nightmarish recollection of the first night after our arrival, after the soldiers opened the doors of the cars—

HS: Of the cattle cars.

NM: —several beatings and thefts ensued. My father had been warned about the deportations by a Romanian officer. He advised him to be careful, to not take too many things, since he would have to cover large distances on foot and he had two small children in tow. Take only heavy clothing, he said, and money or other valuable objects you can use to save yourself. But don't take large suitcases. They'll only weigh you down.
I remember that night, and I remember afterward, living with many families in a small room, in a kind of chaotic panic.

HS: The camps in Transnistria were run by Romanians, weren't they?

NM: The majority of them were run by Romanians, particularly in the south. Farther north, camps were occasionally run by Germans. It was almost impossible to escape from those camps. Corruption was rampant among the Romanians. The danger was more chaotic, less predictable. Brute violence might erupt at any moment, on a clear blue day. The Germans, on the other hand, were disciplined. If they were ordered not to kill, they didn't kill. If they were ordered to kill, they murdered in an orderly and efficient manner. We were under the Romanians.

HS: There was a 50 percent mortality rate in the Transnistrian camps.

NM: Right, and the greatest number of deaths occurred at the beginning, during the first or second winter. Then, starting in 1942 or 1943, the war situation became more equivocal. After Stalingrad, the Romanians—ever adaptable and opportunistic—understood that the war might not be won. There was no longer a foreseeable outcome, and they realized they might be held accountable for deporting the Jews. Consequently the Jews were treated less harshly. They were given the opportunity to work in factories. My father worked, and earned a little bit to eat. Edgar Hilsenrath describes this type of camp very well in his book *The Night.* They didn't burn you in a crematorium. They didn't necessarily kill you. You would die of illness, of hunger . . .

HS: Or because a guard couldn't stand you, or when, out of the blue, he'd just start shooting at random.

NM: Exactly. Or because someone would decide to amuse himself: "Let's have us a slaughter today! That'll be fun!" They took to murder willingly, as we know, and liked to humiliate their victims first. Beyond these sinister episodes, everything was uncertain and chaotic. There was a large black market too, the kind Hilsenrath describes in his book. For an apple you'd trade a ring, or a pair of shoes, or anything you had left.

HS: Your father had money with him that he'd saved to buy a house, didn't he?

NM: Yes, like most young couples, he and my mother struggled to accumulate some savings. The first shock awaited them when we arrived at the Dniester, on the border between Romania and Ukraine. There was an office there where they could exchange Romanian money for German marks. Only these weren't the marks that circulated in Germany; they were valid only in occupied territories. Half the value of the money would be lost in the exchange. Later on, when I asked her about this period in her life, my mother told me a Romanian officer had warned her, "Don't exchange anything here. You'll lose it all." The exchange rate on the other side of the Dniester was much more advantageous.

Mother used a large part of the money to rent a cart for my grandparents. They couldn't walk. They were already old, as I am now.

HS: These were your mother's parents.

NM: Yes. My mother felt closer to her parents than did her brothers and sisters. She was the favorite daughter, the youngest. And that's how the grandparents came with us. They died of typhus soon after arriving in camp, however, in spite of her huge efforts to save them.

HS: What happened to your father's family?

NM: Most of them were not deported. The Jews who *were* deported

13

were from Bukovina and Bessarabia. Racial laws were in effect in Muntenia and Moldova, in the western part of the country, but Jews from there weren't deported. In Transylvania, which—after the second Vienna Diktat—was under Hungarian rule, the Jews were deported to Auschwitz in 1944.

HS: This was after the Arrow Cross Party, the national socialist party, staged a coup d'état in Hungary and removed Admiral Horthy from power.

NM: Correct. Elie Wiesel was one of those Jews. Jews from the middle of the country—from Muntenia and Moldova—suffered as well, as we know from the journal Mihail Sebastian kept in Bucharest,[1] but they were not deported. Deportation was more of a threat to keep them in a state of permanent terror. Some of them were sent to work camps, but they were not deported to Transnistria.

HS: How long were you in the camp?

NM: Starting in October 1941. We returned to Romania in April 1945. But for the last year, approximately, we lived under the Russians. We were liberated by the Soviet Army, and we stayed there until they allowed us to return to Romania.

---

1 See Mihail Sebastian. *Journal 1935-1944: The Fascist Years*. Random House (2012); Rowman and Littlefield (2012).

–PART TWO–
The Moment of Liberation

HS: Do you remember the Soviet Army?

NM: Very well. I wasn't a child anymore. At eight years old, I was already an old man. When the Russians reached us we were in Moghilev, a relatively important city in Ukraine.

HS: Were you still in the camp?

NM: It was a kind of ghetto, I think. There were no windows or doors in the houses. The Romanian army was all around. They weren't in the business of building special camps for us.

HS: Were you surrounded by barbed wire?

NM: In some places, yes. In others, no. In our case, there wasn't barbed wire.

In Transnistria there were three children who later became writers: myself, age five; Aharon Appelfeld, age eight; and Edgar Hilsenrath, who was fourteen or fifteen. That's a huge difference in age! Hilsenrath has a clear picture of the situation; Appelfeld's is, to some extent, less clear, but in any case clearer than mine.

HS: How did you experience the moment of liberation?

NM: The Russians arrived at night. The Germans had already withdrawn in a great panic.

HS: And the Romanians?

N.S.: I think they had already withdrawn at an earlier time. When the Russians arrived, the Romanians were no longer there. And the Germans, as I've said, had retreated in a huge panic. There were two bridges over the Dniester, one made of wood, the other of steel. A little before midnight we heard a sudden fanfare, a brass band playing a kind of funeral march. We were afraid we would be liquidated at the last moment by the Germans—or by the Ukrainians. Back then, Ukrainian volunteers could be even more dangerous than the Germans.

So we were frightened, and we didn't know what that music was meant to signal. After a few minutes, the music stopped, and we heard a powerful explosion. The bridges exploded. First one, then the other. The scene was hellish: motor vehicles, tanks, and other conveyances stood on either side of the leveled bridge while others lay in the water. Germans were caught on both sides of the river. There was an exchange of artillery fire. It was a very frightening, anxious night. Guess who showed up the next morning while everyone was waiting for the victorious Soviet Army.

HS: You tell me.

NM: A group of partisans on horseback. They were the army's advance guard, total youngsters. It was almost comic that the Germans had run away from these young partisans. They looked like a bunch of amateurs, volunteers—which is what they were, in fact. But they weren't exactly dilettantes in battle.

Some Germans had remained in the city. It was very dangerous to go out of the house. There were exchanges of gunfire all the time. Abandoned carriages, cars and trucks lay strewn all over the city; clothes, chocolate, canned goods—everything the army had—was mixed in with explosives. People ran to get the food and were killed on the spot.

HS: Were the partisans in uniform?

NM: The closest thing they had to uniforms were automatic pistols, weapons with drum-shaped loaders, Kalashnikovs. Besides those, the flatbed trucks with Katyusha rocket loaders were certainly impressive. They devastated the Germans on the other side of the river.

HS: Were there Jews among the partisans?

NM: So it seems. And there were many Jews in the army too—officers as well as enlisted men.

HS: How did the Russians treat you? Were there any incidents of rape?

NM: I don't remember. It's possible. In any event, it wasn't a matter of occupying Germany but of liberating Ukraine, which was Soviet territory. Who would the Russians rape? Ukrainian women? It wasn't as if the soldiers had entered enemy territory and were looking for vengeance. As for us, they didn't touch us.

HS: So the arrival of the Soviet Army came as a great relief to you.

NM: The real terror was over, but the Russians immediately enlisted the men—including my father—and sent them to the front line.

HS: Was he happy about that? I ask because the Americans put a gun in a friend of mine's hand after liberating him from a camp. In American uniform he finally had the chance to defend himself against his enemy. For him, being armed was the happiest moment of his life. Of course, my friend was young at the time. He hadn't turned twenty yet.

NM: My father didn't like it. The men were emaciated after all those years in the camps. They were completely unprepared. In truth, they were sent to the front to die. That was as clear as could be. My father was thirty-six years old. He had a wife and two children. He was depressed and exhausted.

HS: He was thirty-six going on sixty-three.

NM: Right, and that's why he ran away from the army.

HS: How did he escape?

NM: He and a comrade of his took off and hid for days on end in the woods. Meanwhile, my mother felt as if she had to move us to the south of Bessarabia, closer to Romania, where we were reunited with my father by sheer luck after his having fled through the woods. In Bessarabia my father worked in a Soviet bank. He learned Russian and Ukrainian quickly. And I was enrolled in a Russian school.

HS: Did they hang Stalin's photo on the wall?

NM: Probably, but my memories about that school don't revolve around him. I recall two details in particular: the red neckerchiefs that we received as young pioneers, and a classmate, Maia—a beautiful blond girl, the daughter of an important officer—wrapping her books and notebooks in wonderful shiny red or yellow paper, unlike the rest of us ordinary mortals.

HS: How big was your class?

NM: Twenty-five or thirty children. Boys and girls.

HS: How many were Jews?

NM: Several.

HS: How Jewish, in fact, was your household? Did you fast on Yom Kippur? Did you celebrate Pesach? Did you keep kosher?

NM: My parents fasted on Yom Kippur, but I went to school on the holiday. In the meantime I had become a zealous young communist after the war. I recall that my grandfather was a very religious man. My mother remained a traditional Jewish woman and a very Jewish mother. Our house wasn't kosher. However, every Pesach she did a complete spring cleaning. My mother wouldn't eat dairy products with meat, nor did she eat pork, but otherwise she wasn't strictly observant, and she allowed us to eat all kinds of food. She used to say that pork wasn't good for her, that it made her sick, that this had probably become a biological reaction over time. I grew up in a traditional—though hardly rigorous—Jewish home, both before and after the camp.

–THE THIRD DIALOGUE–
On Happiness

HS: Then, in April 1945, you returned to Romania, to the place where you spent your childhood?

NM: No. In Iţcani, Suceava—the place from which we'd set out—nothing remained of what we'd left. We had nothing to return to. We came back to a city in the vicinity, to Fălticeni, not in Bukovina, but more to the south. My grandfather on my father's side lived there, my father's brother, and other relatives who had not been deported. We lived there for three months, and then we moved back to Bukovina, but to Rădăuţi.

HS: The hometown of Dan Pagis, the great poet of Israel.

NM: My father found work at Rădăuţi. He was an accountant. And I was a happy child!

HS: Why?

NM: I had everything: school, classmates. Rădăuţi was a pleasant city. A lot of parks, gardens, and greenery. The atmosphere was very animated right after the war. We were like newborns. And I was a good student.

HS: You liked it at school?

NM: Very much. I remember my elementary school teacher even now. She had a Ukrainian name, Vera Iurashok. At her house I celebrated Christmas for the first time. I was her favorite student. I had my hair shaved down to skin—

HS: Because of lice?

NM: No, that was the school rule. All the pupils had shaved heads. I remember that evening. I felt very bashful. There was a festive, mystic atmosphere that I didn't understand. They treated me very well because the teacher liked me. I assume she had told the guests that I was a good student and a Jewish child who had survived the Nazi camps. I don't know. In any case, they were all very kind to me—and cautious, as if I were made of glass and they didn't want to break me. It was exciting, but intimidating at the same time. I was seeing a traditional Christmas meal for the first time, traditional ornaments. When my parents asked me afterward how it was, I couldn't answer. I was feeling a bit guilty that I'd been in this odd foreign place—at those bizarre festivities that were cheerful, and mystic too—without knowing anything about Jesus and the ritual of Christmas. I was ten years old back then, and the teacher was really wonderful, enchanting.

HS: Let's talk about Dan Pagis.

NM: I didn't know him at Rădăuţi. At the age of 13, I was already living in Suceava again, the city of my birth. There we met our housekeeper again. She was an unusual member of our family. Honest—very honest—and very devoted. She loved us and we loved her. She followed us to the camp and brought us food and clothing. She knew our relatives who had not been deported; she sent them letters to ask for money to help us, which was forbidden. She was arrested, and went through a lot of trouble because she helped us. Maria was a Christian of peasant origin, an orphan child who had been taken into my grandfather's house and who grew to be a wonderful woman—and a very beautiful one—a heroine without honors who herself ended up a victim of communism. Before the deportation she took care of me, not my mother. Between us there was a special relationship. I loved her very much and she loved me. I was her prince.

In 1947, when we returned to our city, she was first lady, the wife of the city's First Secretary for Suceava. It was a great shock for us! Her husband, the big communist, invited my father for a talk. He said to him, "I know everything about you. My wife told me you are a good man—honest, generous. I know what you have done for her. I know that Maria was considered a real member of your family, not a housekeeper, so I consider you one of ours. We are building a new society, and your place is by our side." My father, who had never been interested in politics, capitulated. Eventually he became the director of commercial enterprise, a relatively important function in a little city. He also wound up in a communist jail in the end—but that's another story.

The communist fairy tale excited me at the ripe old age of thirteen. I must mention, however, that before this I had been a "Betarist" in Rădăuți, a young adoptee of Ze'ev Jabotinski, the founder of rightist "revisionist" Zionism, who was born in Odessa and died in America in 1940. I was strongly convinced that we must abandon ghetto mentality and Diaspora habits, that we should go back "home" to the Holy Land and build our own society to prove that we were no longer a bunch of cowards, forever humiliated by others. I was very enthusiastic. Another lovely fairy tale for the young survivor.

HS: Where did all this come from?

NM: There was a powerful Jewish community in Rădăuți. There were Zionist organizations from the extreme right to the extreme left, and ferocious debates raged between them, quarrels, everything you needed to cook up Jewish madness. After the war, the dispute was carried on with unusual passion. The question was being asked, what should we do now? Should we stay? Should we emigrate? Some thought that in Romania everything would change for the better; others saw no future there. I remember this febrile phase of post-war, post-camp childhood, and all the Zionist organizations, *Hanoar Hatzioni*, *Gordonia*, *Hashomer Hatzair*, and naturally *Betar*, the organization I belonged to. Why did I join? Because Betar was the most powerful Zionist organization in Rădăuți, and because it had an impressive project for the future.

HS: What organization did Dan Pagis belong to?

NM: I don't know. He only stayed a short time in Rădăuți. I didn't know him personally.

HS: Isn't that ironic? When you were a child you belonged to the Betar organization, yet you remained in Romania, while Dan Pagis—who may not have belonged to any Zionist organization—immigrated to Israel and entered a kibbutz.

NM: In the course of our dialogue, we'll run into many paradoxes like that. The difference between Dan Pagis and me lies in the fact that he was an orphan. I returned to Romania with my parents. In this regard, I wasn't able personally to decide if we would emigrate or not. When my parents heard my soaring pleas for emigration, they'd only smile and say, "Let's see. Let's wait. Nothing's rushing us."

One day, my father's younger sister, a convinced Betarist herself, came to us with steamship tickets. That was in 1946. My father said, "I'm too tired. I've just unpacked. I can't pack again."

HS: If your father had made another decision, you would have been an Israeli citizen today. Can you imagine that?

NM: Certainly. I have classmates from Rădăuți, and also from Suceava, who have been in Israel for a long time.

HS: In one of your books you recount an anecdote about four friends. One lives in Tel Aviv, another in New York, the third in Buenos Aires. And the fourth? The fourth is an adventurer: He lives in Bucharest. Are you…

NM: Yes, I am the adventurer.

–THE FOURTH DIALOGUE–
Comrade Stalin

HS: How did the Betarist transform himself into a communist?

NM: It was a matter of passing from one story to another. Both were about "the new man," about the "the new Jew," or *the new man* in the universal sense. Socialist Educational Reform took place when I was a student at the Jewish Lycée Suceava, at the end of 1947. All private schools were prohibited. They became state schools. The Communist Pioneer Organization was set up in 1949. I was the commandant of this organization in my school because I was a good student, the class prizewinner—already a bad sign for my future life! Thus began my career as a communist. I had become a kind of star. I was short, not very athletic, but I gave speeches on November seventh (the anniversary of Russia's October Revolution, a festive day with parades) and on the first of May, and so on and so forth. In 1949, when Stalin celebrated his 70th birthday, in my capacity as commandant of Pioneers I wrote him a letter and a poem—I along with many other comrades in ideas: Neruda, Aragon, Anna Seghers, Roger Garaudy. With everyone else, I congratulated the genius, our divine and spiritual father, grandfather and great-grandfather. My older comrades' messages were infantile; I, however, was a child in fact. In 1950 I entered the lycée.

HS: It wasn't the Jewish Lycée any longer, but a state school.

NM: Yes. There, after several years, I became the secretary of the Union of Communist Youth (UTC), then known as the Union of Working Youth (*UTM*, in Romanian). The Communist Party itself was then called the Romanian Workers' Party (*PMR* in Romanian).

HS: Did you read Marxist classics at that time?

NM: Of course. I was a passionate reader! I read *The Communist Manifesto*, Engels' *Anti-Dühring*.

HS: *Das Capital?*

NM: No. I didn't read *Das Capital*, I'm sorry, but I did read Lenin's *One Step Forward, Two Steps Back*; Stalin's *Problems of Leninism*; Lenin's *The State and Revolution*. I read a ton of throwaways too, Soviet literature.

HS: Sholokhov?

NM: Sholokhov is a good writer in comparison with the pearls of Socialist realism. I read his *And Quiet Flows the Don* with great pleasure. I was referring only to the real trash. But I also read classic Russian literature, wonderfully translated into Romanian: Tolstoy, Chekov, Turgenev, Gogol, Pushkin, Goncharov…

HS: Dostoyevsky?

NM: Dostoyevsky was only partially available back then. I was only just able to read him in the '60s. It was the same with modern Western literature, also Isaak Babel. I was reading good Russian literature. It protected me in some measure from the stupidity of the Socialist-realist phrases and clichés I was consuming.

HS: When did you learn to read, in fact?

NM: Russian between 1944 and 1945, Romanian only in 1945. My parents taught me a bit before that. When we returned I went to the "Israelite School" in Fălticeni, where my paternal grandfather and other relatives lived. It wasn't a secondary school; it was a primary one. The school's director was my mother's cousin. I went directly into the second grade, and on graduating I numbered among the best—a dubious achievement, as I would later understand. I was very diligent. After all we'd lived through until then, it was a real Paradise for me to find myself in a classroom, with teachers, books, notebooks, pencils, games, and a playground. I met aunts who spoiled me, cooked for me. All of a sudden I had been transformed into a kind of prince. More exactly, I had returned to being the prince I had been until the age of 5, before I was transformed into a beggar and prisoner, a bug or insect.

So I began to read, and I was fascinated by books. The first book I came across was a collection of Romanian fairy tales. I received it on July 19, 1945, for my birthday, at the solemn age of nine. I remember it had a green pasteboard cover. Its author was a great Romanian storyteller, Ion Creanga. The book was written in a peculiar and fascinating tongue, not in street slang. The language was archaic, popular, original, wonderful. I was captivated by this different world, by this different language. This was my entry into the world of literature, into the unreal world of the real. And in this way I became a passionate reader. I'd read everything that fell into my hands.

HS: Let's return to comrade Stalin.

NM: When he died in 1953, I'd already moved away from him. I was still the UTM secretary at the boys' lycée, and I knew the secretary of the girls' lycée very well. When Stalin died, she cried like a madwoman. You'd swear she was ready to die from one moment to the next. She was destroyed. She'd lost her daddy, her grandfather, her god. I didn't cry. I had already realized the dubiousness of the atmosphere back then. I had begun to understand the double talk.

HS: What happened between you and Stalin?

NM: A simulacrum of a trial in which I had to "unmask" and exclude several students from the youth organization had taken place at the lycée. A little Stalinist trial, painful for me. I couldn't stand myself any more in the position of a little Stalin, which was probably how a poor UTM secretary was seen in those days.

HS: What happened, more precisely?

NM: Do you know who Ana Pauker was?

HS: No.

NM: Ana Pauker was an important figure in Romanian Communism—perhaps the most important Romanian figure on the international communist scene. Her trial in the 30's, when she was condemned to ten years in prison, was on the first pages of European newspapers. She was called a "new Pasionaria," which is to say that she was compared with Dolores Ibárruri, the legendary Spanish communist. Ana Pauker came from a very religious family, and a very poor one. Her grandfather was a rabbi. He very early understood how intelligent she was. He managed to slip her into a cheyder, a religious preparatory school for Jewish boys, although this was forbidden. She proved an excellent pupil, brilliant even in childhood. In her youth she worked as an apprentice tailor, then as a Hebrew teacher at a school. One day she saw an anti-Semitic demonstration. She went home and didn't speak another word with anyone for a week. Then she joined the labor movement, and later the Communist Party. There she met her future husband, Marcel Pauker (her maiden name was Rabinsohn, Hannah Rabinsohn). He was among the founders of the Communist Party, and he came from a wealthy Jewish family. He had studied in Switzerland, where he graduated with a degree in engineering. They married, and they had two children. Marcel Pauker was an agent of the Komintern, as was Ana. During the years when she was in prison, he stayed with the children—in Switzerland, in Austria, anywhere the party sent him. Then he was suddenly called to Moscow.

HS: This happened by 1937?

NM: In that period. All his friends advised him not to go. It was a turbulent time. No one knew what was going to happen. Pauker replied, "I'm crystal clean." He left with the two children. They stayed in the famous Hotel Lux, reserved for foreign militants, and right after his arrival he was brought in for interrogation. His children were taken and placed in an orphanage. He was left alone for a while, and worked as an engineer. Then he was arrested again, and executed. Ana was still in a women's prison in Romania. The party instructed her to gather the communist detainees in prison and to condemn Marcel Pauker as a Trotskyite, a traitor who abused the party's trust and who had received the proper punishment. She refused for three days, saying she knew him too well, and she couldn't believe these accusations. Then she did as she had been ordered. If the party said he had been a Trotskyite, probably he had been.

Then the Soviet Union offered Romania an exchange of prisoners: a Romanian spy who had been arrested in the Soviet Union in exchange for Ana Pauker. And so Ana Pauker arrived in Moscow.

HS: In what year did this happen?

NM: In 1939, I believe. A friend of hers, an important party functionary, waited for her at the airport to warned her, "There is one subject about which you are not allowed to discuss with anyone, ever: your husband." She got her children out of the orphanage and worked for the party in the Soviet Union during the war. There she formed a division of Romanian war prisoners to fight against the Germans. As a matter of fact, the Romanian communist brigade during the Spanish Civil was called the Ana Pauker Brigade. I mention this so that you realize how important she was.

In 1944 she returned to Romania. Rumor has it she may have been waited for by a small delegation of party functionaries, who would have told her, "You are our most important comrade, but a woman, and a Jew on top of that. As party leader in an Orthodox Christian country, this isn't going to work. Consequently, our leader will remain Gheorghiu-Dej, but you will be the real leader, in fact." Pauker accepted, and became the *éminence grise*, number two after Gheorghiu-Dej.

She had a sister and two brothers. Both sisters were convinced communists, while the two brothers were convinced religious Zionists. They maintained good relations despite their ideological differences, and she felt especially close to one of her brothers. After the war, when this brother was already in Israel, she implored him to come back to Romania, "Come here. Return." He responded, "Why should I come back? Romania is a communist country. I have no business being there." She insisted: "I am here, and I love you, and I need you." Poor guy, he went back.

It's interesting to mention that she was the one who, on returning from the Soviet Union, looked first for her in-laws, the parents of the Trotskyite and traitor executed by the Soviet comrades. In her villa in Bucharest—guarded by soldiers and police, in an isolated, privileged neighborhood—there was a special room for her brother, who wore *peyes* and a black hat, like all the ultra orthodox Jews. The guard at the gate knew that this was comrade Ana's brother. By 1952, as in all the countries dominated by the Soviets, the situation inside the Communist Party had grown tense—mobilized for unmasking "deviationists." It was the era of trials, with cases against Rudolf Slánsky, and László Rajik, and Kostov. And Ana Pauker was accused of a heresy called "leftist and rightist deviations." Left and right at the same time! Might this be typically Romanian?

HS: Are we possibly looking at an example of the phenomenon that the educated Marxist calls "dialectic"?

NM: Mmmm, yeah. Left and right at the same time? Very Byzantine, and terribly "dialectic," if you will. Ana Pauker had to become a victim. A delegation of Romanian Communists lead by Gheorghiu Dej travelled to Moscow for approval. She was too important, too visible, to simply be arrested without the blessing of the communist Vatican—particularly because she was considered Stalin's "favorite child." The Pope Joseph Vissarionovich approved—with a certain satisfaction, it seems. Ana knew very well how these farces unfolded in the Land of Victorious Socialism (and not just there). She had the experience of her husband's murder. Accusations were invented and put together in high-level bureaus. In her case, it was stated that she had been against the collectivization of agriculture, and aspired to a Titoist political solution. She was arrested and interrogated, accused of being an agent of the Israelis and Americans. Then Stalin died. The interrogations were interrupted, and she was visited in her cell by one of the new party secretaries, who said to her, "I'm bringing you the news that comrade Stalin has died." Comrade Ana collapsed in grief. The new secretary hastened to console her: "Ana, his death has saved you!"

She was freed and given a job as editor at a political publishing house. She never went there. She stayed at home and read like a madwoman. Then she became ill with cancer, and died. That's the story of Hannah Rabinsohn. Although she disappeared in the '50s, her name is often recalled—even today—in Romania when they talk about the "Jewish-communist conspiracy." In this context she's called Hannah Rabinsohn, not Ana Pauker—as if Pauker were a name on the order of Gheorghiu, Ceauşescu, Iliescu. Her maiden name shows that she was part of the old rabbinic conspiracy of the Elders of Zion, and her husband's name shows that she was part of the Jewish communist conspiracy.

HS: Do you think she was a heroine?

NM: She certainly wasn't an angel. She did and approved horrible things, same as Marcel Pauker, Trotsky, Kaganovici, Slánsky, Mátyas Rákosi, and others. They were the party's disciplined Jewish soldiers and pupils. They did everything in the name of the party, not in the name of a Talmudic conspiracy or for the State of Israel. Ana Pauker was a real, believing communist. Her deeds were communist, from first to last. But in Romania, in anti-Semitic writings even today, she remains a symbol of the Jewish evil.

Recently, a Romanian magazine asked me to speak about Romanian anti-Semitism. I wrote as follows:

"I don't know to what extent it will be useful to tell the rhinoceroses that, as the result of my prolonged Bolshevik activities, when I was five years old I was deported to Transnistria, from whence I returned at the age of nine in 1945. On this occasion, I brought the Soviet tanks that installed Jewish Communism in Romania. The first thing I did when I entered again into possession of my country was to convince my circumcised comrades to change their Jewish names to Romanian ones: Gidale Deutsch would become Gheorghiu-Dej; Bodinger would be Bodnăras; Vily Lister would be Vasile Luca; Motel would be Moghioroş; Leiba Polanski would be Lucreţiu Pătrăşcanu; Sami Clein would be Chivu Stoica; Gold Asher would be Gheorghe Apostol; Nahum Ceauşu would be Nicolae Ceauşescu; Itsic Itscovich would become Ion Iliescu; and so on and so forth, the better to fool the oppressed masses. As a consequence of my racial and ideological prejudices, I did not take part in the large anti-communist resistance in Romania lead by comrade Corneliu (whose family name was Codreanu in a former life)[2], former court poet to N. Ceauşescu and serving today in the European Parliament under the name of Corneliu Vadim Tudor. For this I ask the forgiveness of the all-merciful Romanian people."

My note never appeared in print.

HS: Very witty. But tell me, though, what happened to the brother of Ana Pauker.

NM: He went back to Israel after he recollected himself for several years in Romanian communist prisons.

HS: Let's talk again about what you lived through in the '50s.

NM: In the period of "leftist and rightist" deviations, I was the UTM secretary at my lycée. I was informed by the city's activists that I would have to expel at least three members from the organization.

---

2 Corneliu Zelea Codreanu was the founder of the Iron Guard.

HS: Who told you that?

NM: An activist came from the city leadership of the UTM organization. He told me that I would have to organize a big meeting—like the ones that were taking place back then in all the factories, state enterprises, and hospitals—in order to enthusiastically sustain the Central Committee's decision regarding deviation, thus cleansing the party of traitors and saboteurs. The idea was that there were traitors all over the place—in your lycée, in your hospital, in your sports club—everywhere! That's how the great purification began.

Accordingly, I was given the task of "purifying" our organization of at least three suspect students. And after much discussion the names of three guiltless individuals were proposed. One of them was of peasant origin. His father hadn't agreed with the idea of entering the collective farm—proof that he was an enemy of the party and the state. The other was an absolutely inoffensive Jew, son of a butcher. His father still had a sort of partially private store, and his guilt was passed to his offspring. The third was my friend. I admired him. He was one grade ahead of me, civilized; his father had once been a liberal lawyer. The father had been locked up for two years. By then he had already been freed. Two years in prison meant that they had found absolutely nothing against him, that he was absolutely clean.

HS: What happened to the three boys?

NM: They graduated from lycée without being members of UTM. They weren't thrown out of school. I don't know what happened to the peasant's son. He was in a lower grade. The other two went to the university. The Jewish boy studied veterinary medicine and lives in Israel today, while my friend enrolled in the same faculty as I, though not in Bucharest. But he didn't graduate. This failure was his great accomplishment.

HS: Why?

NM: He became a solitary, almost aristocratic failure. An ordinary functionary, he kept his life private and his library private, and his solitude. I visited him often when I lived in Romania, and also afterwards. He remained unchanged.

NM: And you?

NM: I didn't suffer at all when comrade Stalin left me. I had already separated from him. I graduated from the lycée and I went on to university. Because my scholastic results were very good—grades, political activities—it was proposed that I be part of the UTM leadership in my first year on faculty. I refused. The fellow who conducted the session would become Romania's foreign minister after several years. The repercussions were modest: I had to present myself to the leadership of UTM in the capital, where I was harshly criticized.

HS: Were you ever a member of the Communist Party?

NM: No. Never.

–THE FIFTH DIALOGUE–
The Jewish Monopoly

HS: When did you become a writer?

NM: With the publication of my first book.

HS: No, that's not what I meant to say. When did you sit down, pencil in hand for the first time in front of a blank page, and start writing?

NM: Very early. I wrote poems in adolescence.

HS: Were they rhymed poems?

NM: Rhymed poems, but also blank verse.

HS: That's bourgeois formalism, comrade!

NM: Yes, a stimulating formalism, though—even courageous, under Socialist conditions. I began to write seriously when I got to the university. It was a long, bumpy process, not a continuous preoccupation. In 1966 I sent several short stories to a poet—Miron Radu Paraschivescu, called MRP for short. What I knew about him was, he had the best nose for discovering talent, a cultivated, intelligent person with a sure sense of literature, and great knowledge. He was enthusiastic.

HS: What was your poetry about? What did it talk about?

NM: Solitude. A very decadent theme. I reread the poems after some time . . .

HS: So that you could see if they were good for anything.

NM: Some of the poems were bearable. They weren't brilliant, but in them I recaptured a tone belonging to Romanian interwar poetry—a turmoil of loneliness, a search for something beyond the oppressive daily round—this in contrast to what was being published in literary reviews. If these verses had literary value I don't know, but if they had been published back then I don't think I would have been ashamed.

HS: What was your prose about?

NM: The first prose texts were impressions, fragments from childhood in the camp, a transfiguration of what I'd experienced.

HS: Had you talked with friends back then about what you'd gone through?

NM: No.

HS: As a result you conducted a dialogue with a sheet of white paper.

NM: Yes. Just that. It was a great shock for me when I came to America and discovered that this theme—

HS: When you say "this theme," you're referring to the so-called Holocaust?

NM: —that this topic is so present here, in the public domain. It's spoken about. Personal experiences are recounted. At the beginning I was extremely reluctant, and I didn't feel comfortable about the public exhibition of suffering.

HS: It was too personal for you.

NM: Yes, it was personal. But after a while I reconsidered, to an extent. That is, I began to respond to questions that were put to me about my biography. Here, public exposure is almost inevitable. If this chapter existed in your life, then you'd have to answer some questions; it's an accepted ritual. Over there, no one would ask you. The manipulated falsity of public life—everything was more or less falsified—would make you hide inside yourself—to defend, at least, the integrity of private life, your only private territory, the property that you wanted kept safe from the public lie. Here in the United States, the situation was and is different, although resemblances exist. The difference is that the ubiquitous hunter is no longer the Party but the wild beast of the scandal-seeking mass media, which is increasingly dominant everywhere.

The first stories spoke of childhood. Then I wrote about the communist period as well, about the years when I was a dreamy young enthusiast. It is interesting that in recent years Romanians have reproached me for having written only about the Holocaust, although my texts about the Holocaust are few compared with those about communism. I have discussed this with Imre Kertész and Aharon Appelfeld, who was sometimes criticized in Israel because Israel doesn't appear enough in his work. I have remained preoccupied, in fact, with the theme of alienation, of oppression, and discomfort, wherever they may be discovered: in Nazi camps, under communism, in exile. This continuity transcends the social, political, and historic framework. It is a matter of the tension between the individual and the surrounding social context.

HS: Who in Romania reproached you that you had written only about the Holocaust?

NM: Under the communists it was a taboo topic. I recall a blurb on the cover of one of my books that said that I belonged to a generation "that had an unhappy childhood during the war."

HS: "An unhappy childhood during the war." That's great.

NM: It was simply impossible to call things by name. After the collapse of Communism, everything began to come to the surface. One of the most heated debates after 1989—one which goes on from time to time even now, though with less force, and in which I was involved, with or without my willing it—involved comparing the Gulag and the Holocaust. Suddenly it was possible to talk about the Holocaust, a topic that met with jamming right away. Part of the Romanian intellectual elite was asking, "Why the Holocaust? Did we really just escape the Holocaust, or Communism? We find ourselves somehow in 1945. The camps were liberated yesterday . . . Or is it the case that the communist dictatorship just collapsed, and we should be debating everything we went through under it?"

HS: So an immediate collision of memories took place.

NM: Yes, right away, a huge collision, with the revival of anti-Semitic slogans from before the war to which new ingredients were added: "The Jews brought us communism"; "There was no Holocaust in Romania. That's just a lie."; "There was no Auschwitz in our country. The whole thing is an exaggeration, a falsification, Jewish propaganda, a Jewish-Israeli plot." An important personality in the literary world— currently president of the Writers' Union—uttered a critical pronouncement directed at "the Jewish monopoly on suffering." We're dealing here not with an anti-Semite but with a democrat—a smart, well-read, cultivated man. That's the big surprise. The formula doesn't betray much compassion, or understanding of one's own history, or solidarity with the oppressed, or an excess of intelligence and honesty, either. And as I say, this is not a matter of some ferocious nationalist and anti-Semite, but of a respected intellectual, and a democrat. Voila! This time the formula doesn't come from the nationalistic periphery of intellectual life, but from the center of the intellectual elite!

In this context, the Garaudy case becomes very interesting, on account of its echo in Romania. Roger Garaudy was a leading member of the French Communist Party. For a while he was even in the Political Bureau, and ideological chief of the party. He had a very peculiar evolution, I'd say. In the '60s he became a liberal communist, aligning himself with so-called Euro-Communism. Ultimately he was excluded from the party. He was always close to the Church, and then he became Catholic, and later Protestant. In the end he converted to Islam. Garaudy wrote a book entitled *Founding Myths of Modern Israel*. He's a furious anti-Zionist. I believe he became anti-Semitic as well.

HS: Garaudy denies the genocide committed against the Jews of Europe.

NM: He declares that the number of victims isn't as large as the Jews say, and believes there were no gas chambers. He was condemned in Paris before an audience of noisy anti-Semites, many of them Muslims, who kept shouting, "Death to the Jews."

HS: When did this trial take place?

NM: In 1998. After Roger Garaudy's book appeared at a miniscule press belonging to the extreme right—whose owner had ties to Romania, in fact—the condemned author became a cause célèbre in the Islamic world. The vice-president of Syria dubbed him "the greatest contemporary occidental philosopher." Muammar al-Gaddafi declared him "the greatest European philosopher since Plato and Aristotle." The hero was received by the notables of the Islamic Republic of Iran, and even Hassan Nasrallah, the Hezbollah chief, appreciated Garaudy enthusiastically.

HS: What is the connection to Romania?

NM: We might well ask. If we follow the Romanian debate, which became disgusting rather quickly, it has to do with certain illustrious members of the intellectual elite. I was put in a corner for my stand on this issue. Two principal ideas could be distinguished in the confused unleashing of resentments: First, that Jews were ready to commit any falsification to maintain their "monopoly on suffering." Second, that the expression of an opinion is not a crime or misdemeanor. An opinion isn't an infraction that can be condemned through a process of law. A Romanian newspaper article even affirmed that this legal process against Garaudy would be "the death of Descartes." Nobody was ready to recall the essential fact that the breaking of a French law was under consideration, a law approved by the democratic French state.

The Garaudy trial took place in France in about the same period when the stormy Holocaust/Gulag debate was growing by leaps and bounds in Romania. The Jews, it was said, aren't really interested in the Gulag, because most of them were communists and would do absolutely anything so that the memory of the Holocaust, presented as the greatest genocide in history, would prevail over other historic tragedies. Hence this sudden, post-communist, Romanian interest in Roger Garaudy, formerly a fierce communist, one who used to affirm that every word of Stalin's was true, while all anti-Stalinists are liars. Many Romanians are vehement anti-communists today, but their anti-communism sometimes seems not so much an option for democracy as a new opportunism, or an updated variant of the old nationalism. It's easy to be anti-communist today—and very useful.

HS: Roger Garaudy himself is just a marginal, risible intellectual figure. He doesn't represent anything.

NM: And yet he has an echo. He can be used at need.

–THE SIXTH DIALOGUE–
About Women

HS: I'd like us to go back in time, to talk about the artist as a young man. Allow me to put an indiscreet question in this context: How was it with the ladies?

NM: I didn't know that Mr. Stein was interested in women. But if that's how things stand, I feel suddenly closer to him. When we talk about women, we're also talking about love. But I understand that you want us to talk more about the erotic aspect of the problem.

Women and eroticism are a conjoined theme, but also a private theme. Talking about my youth, we're talking about a period lived in a socialist state. How can you develop a sexual relationship with a woman in a country where people live crowded into packed dwellings sometimes made for communal use, where there doesn't really exist the possibility of withdrawing into a private space, where abortions aren't permitted and contraceptives don't exist, but proletarian morality does. You couldn't even rent a hotel room. All these encumbrances, impediments, restrictions, and restraints can't kill the instincts, however—or love either. I liked women. I like them now, too, even if I can't allow myself to like them too much anymore. I'm married, and I'm no longer young. Still, woman remains more interesting, I think, more fascinating than man.

In my youth, back when my sexual impulses awoke, what could a teenager do in a small city in which anonymity was almost impossible—a teenager who went to an all-boys' school, who only met girls at revolutionary meetings or at the local movie theater once or twice a week, when it got dark inside and you could finally stroke the young lady's skin? You couldn't invite her for a philosophical discussion in your room that didn't exist. Nothing much could happen. No big deal.

Shall I tell you about vague, incipient erotic experiences? Unfortunately, there were no bordellos. During my lycée years it was very difficult to have a sexual relationship. Even later, in Bucharest, it was difficult. I went to Bucharest contrary to the wishes of my family. My parents wanted to keep me in the vicinity—at Iaşi, the Moldavian capital city—but I was firmly oriented toward

Bucharest. Looking for anonymity. I wanted to escape.

In lycée I was a little star. This helps in relations with girls; they like stars. I got close to some girls. I was friends with several. I had an intense relationship with one of them, only incipiently erotic: kisses, discussions, a bit of feeling up in the dark of the movie theater or the city park. Nothing important. In the last two years of lycée I was with a beautiful Jewish girl whose parents were friends with my family. She left to study in Bucharest; I, the same. We were practically together. Our expeditions, to call them that, generally lead to the border of permissibility and stopped a bit short of that point. She was the *Oy-oy-oy-oy, what will mommy say!* type. Beyond that there were several minor, adjacent events, but no initiation in the true sense of the word. When I finished my engineering studies I had a reputation for being an experienced person, because I was always surrounded by girls and I hung around them all the time. They liked me and I liked them. But that was it.

HS: You were a virginal Casanova, consequently?

NM: Kind of. I was shy and solitary. My dream of liberty—and of sexual freedom as well—was, unfortunately, only an aspiration. I didn't have a stable relationship or experience, just a bit of something here and there. After I graduated—

HS: At what age?

NM: Twenty-three. After graduation I returned to the city of my birth. Socialist restrictions—

HS: Which ones?

NM: At that time in Romania—and not only in Romania, I think—there were "closed" cities where you couldn't live if you didn't have the corresponding "documents." I wanted to remain in Bucharest. That was my hope when I enrolled in the Bucharest Construction Institute. I graduated from a faculty that wasn't easy at all. We began as 127 students. Twenty-six of us graduated. I understood quickly enough that I am not cut out for the study of engineering, and yet I carried on. This is my curse: I can't leave anything without making huge efforts. People, habits, friends, homelands, my mother tongue.

I couldn't remain in Bucharest because I didn't have Bucharest identity papers, which were made available only to those born there or who had married somebody from Bucharest. I had offers from other cities, but they didn't attract me. I wanted to live in Bucharest. When I saw, after the graduation exam, that I couldn't remain, I went back to my native city. And I soon fell in love with a girl, a student at the lycée. She became the complete experience for me: emotional, erotic, sexual. A dramatic relationship.

HS: Let me guess: The small fly in the ointment was that she was a *shicksa*, a non-Jew. I'm not using the word *shicksa* in a pejorative or hostile sense; the slang term includes a delicate irony. So, a *shicksa*.

NM: The irony could be affectionate, too, not simply delicate, if we think of Martin Buber's wife, or Celan's and Fondane's wives, or Kafka's Milena, or even of Virginia Woolf, the wife of the Jew Leonard Woof, who cared for her like an angel. There are so many other examples. We're only referring here, however, to a charming, intelligent high school girl. For my mother's taste, she was a much too intelligent *shiksa*. To me, she was very attractive, in addition to being mysterious, witty, unpredictable. We were living in a small city. Anonymity was almost impossible. I would arrange with a colleague at work to lend me his room for two hours…. Maybe you're familiar with these things. Or maybe not.

HS: They're not familiar to me. I didn't grow up in a socialist country.

NM: Then you really don't know a thing. And what is more amazing—and more to be "compassionated"—is that you don't even regret that you don't know a thing. In any case, it was an experience that included many of the premises of "real socialism." Very real.

After several years I managed to return to Bucharest—another difficult adventure. From a political point of view, I no longer had my file in order as it was when I was secretary of the UTM at my lycée. Whenever I managed to find work, I was rejected in the end because of my personnel file. At a certain moment I competed for a position at an important design institute in Bucharest, IPROMET—without having the magic Bucharest I.D.! Already at that time there nevertheless existed conditions for obtaining this great prize if the hiring institution were suffieciently powerful and important to receive a special order from the minister of the respective economic branch. It was called a "ministerial order." After I took the exam for the post, I was promised the "ministerial order." For that, though, I had to bring proof that I had a place to live in Bucharest.

A vicious circle: To live in Bucharest you had to register with the Militia, but if you didn't have Bucharest I.D. you *couldn't* register with the Militia. For the Militia you needed the "ministerial order" in the first place, and then a place to live. You could you have a residence in Bucharest if you were the owner of a place; or if you had a grandfather in Bucharest who left the residence to you in his will, for example; or if someone would declare in court that he or she would accept you "in their dwelling space," and if this space were sufficiently roomy. None of these hypotheticals held true in my case. What does a Jew do in a situation like this? He calls on the solidarity of his community. The power of the "conspiracy," as is well-known, solves any problem. My mother had been a classmate of the wife of the Chief Rabbi of Romania. The women talked things over, and they found a really wonderful solution. The Jewish community had a little space near the *mikveh*. Do you know what a *mikveh* is?

HS: A Jewish pool.

NM: Yes, but for religious women, for their weekly purification before Shabbat or other holidays. The Jewish Community gave me a certificate: I would live in a space in the building with the *mikveh*. And with this document, and with the "ministerial order," I finally received the famous stamp on my I.D.. Shortly after that, I met my future wife. So I could have avoided the entire situation! I entered marriage, however, on a solid legal basis, with my documents in order, as was the affective basis: love. Very old fashioned.

HS: I won't question you about Cella because I see very well that you have a happy marriage, full of love and warmth. It'll be better to go back to the *shicksa*, since this theme is much more dramatic.

NM: We should probably ask Bill Clinton's son-in-law. He's religious person; I'm not. And he loves a *shicksa* and married her although he's the son of a religious Jew—and, it seems, a former financial infractor. That's America!

The son of a Jewish infractor marries the daughter of a former president! And the *shicksa* Chelsea Clinton will bear his children. We could talk about this as a symbolic case, because all the statistics show that in America marriages between Jews and non-Jews produce fewer and fewer children that are considered Jews according to Judaic religious laws. For this reason, the single Jewish community that will remain, like it or not, will be strictly religious. So say the prophets of the day, whether we like it or not. If we don't like it, we can call God on the telephone, because only He can change anything. But He is always very busy—somewhere far away. Some, in fact, maintain that the Holocaust proved that his powers are limited, that He's not really omnipotent.

HS: And your *shicksa* from Romania?

NM: I really loved her. Our relationship gradually became increasingly dramatic and complicated. And for the more religious part of the family, from the Jewish ghetto, the story took on epic proportions: "The dear boy is hypnotized by a diabolic Christian girl!" When I came back to Romania in 1945, a cousin of mine was director of the Jewish school at Fălticeni, and in the meantime he had become a professor of mathematics at the lycée in Suceava. Very agitated by the misfortune that had fallen on our heads, my Jewish mother questioned the professor about his pupil. The cousin told her, "She is the most intelligent girl that I've come across in several generations of students." Instead of being a recommendation in her favor, this seemed to horrify my mother even more.

After much suffering for both of us—but especially for her—we separated; not because of "ethnicities," but because love had gradually consumed its own energy in anxiety.

HS: How long did the relationship last?

NM: Several years. After she graduated university she worked for an important research institute, and at a certain point she left Romania. She married in England. Several years ago, she called me. She had discovered me through my books, and sent me an interesting letter about life after her separation from me. She had two children with her English husband. A month and a half ago, she was here. I tried to prevent the visit, but without success. She kept ringing me and telling me that she wanted to come to New York, that we were both old and we'd soon die. And I would repeat, "No, no, three times no! Let's remain there, let's leave it there, where we were when we were young. You shouldn't see me as I am now, without hair, and with cardiac problems. Nor should I see you, either." But she got stubborn, and came to visit us with her new husband. They're a sympathetic pair.

HS: And?

NM: And nothing.

HS: Nothing?

NM: Nothing. There was not the least bit of tension, though I had expected something like that. In her letter she told me that I should know that she had forgiven me, that I shouldn't have any more guilty feelings. Yes, I did feel guilty. At the end of our frenzied love affair—as happens in cases like these—there was no longer any reason for us to ruin everything. The only thing to do was to let things come to an end. The ruin comes by itself. She was very possessive, dramatic, jealous. There were abortions, too. At a certain moment the whole thing became unbearable. I am ashamed of this ending. I didn't part from her under family pressure, but I was heading toward the end of this love story, and I may have contributed, too, to her ruin.

Paradoxically, when we separated, the hostility of a part of my family had weakened. They had resigned themselves to the inevitable. So they were surprised by this sudden turn of events for which they no longer held out any hope.

She is a woman who stands on her own feet today, with grandchildren. She lives contentedly and securely in England. From my watchtower, our meeting again seems a mistake.

HS: Because there were no longer feelings.

NM We didn't stir up the past. It was a state visit: official, pleasant, civilized. We're old. I am old. I don't know how marriage would have been with her if we had married. Sartre wrote somewhere that the relations between a Jewish man and a non-Jewish woman—sexual, spiritual, intimate, psychological relations—are very different than those with a Jewish woman. In the first case there would be attraction, the temptation of the unknown. He says that the danger of a marriage with a Jewish woman is that love as sexuality evolves into fraternal feelings. It's not really so bad, I would say, if the sexual relationship ends in this kind of love: in friendship, solidarity, reciprocal devotion.

HS: How is it, though, in the other case: when a Jewish woman marries a non-Jew?

NM: We could read Gregor von Rezzori.

HS: Better we should talk about Cella.

NM: As you know, my Jewish wife looks Swedish. When I was with her the first time on vacation at the Black Sea, and we were walking along the edge of the water, we met a former classmate of mine from the Polytechnic Faculty. He whispered to me in passing, "Aha, so this is the kind of woman you're with now! What language do you speak with her?"

–THE SEVENTH DIALOGUE–
Without Glasses in the Camp

HS: Let's talk about completely other things. About your exile, specifically. When did you leave Romania, and why? You held out there for a long time.

NM: As I understand it, there are two questions: Why did I stay so long, and why did I decide to leave?

I stayed so long because I was rooted in the Romanian language. Romanian culture formed me and deformed me. I used to delude myself that I was living in a language, not in a country. In spite of all the unpleasantnesses, the unhappinesses, the problems I was having there—and there were enough of them—I knew that my identity and integrity were linked to the Romanian language, and so to the country. I didn't want to leave; I was skeptical about chasing after luck. In the first place, my instants of fulfillment were moments of reading and writing, moments of solitude. Of course there were other happy moments—when I tried love, or was contemplating the great breadth of the sea, or would meet interesting interlocutors. I didn't see any reason to leave all these things behind, although outside the country there also existed the great promise of having access to books that had been inaccessible to me for 40 years, and of knowing another world, another civilization. But I felt that I'd lose everything as a writer: my roots. In that period I saw exile as suicide for a writer, and there were already many examples to that effect. How could you destroy your lif,e even if you would have pleasanter living conditions?

Why did I leave, though? Because at a certain moment the glass was full to nearly overflowing, and all it needed was one more drop to spill over. In 1986, the year of my departure, the situation in Romania was absolutely unbearable in all aspects of daily life. There was the daily misery, there was the terror, there was the closing of a society that was already very closed anyhow. Back then, even in comparison with the other socialist societies, Romania was in a much worse situation. We had only two hours of television programming. Of these two hours, one hour or more was dedicated to the Leader. And this wasn't happening in Moscow. It was going on in Romania. Romania is not China or Germany. Romania is a Latin country with oriental ingredients. It doesn't support this kind of "sobriety," so to speak. And the anti-Semitism was getting more obvious.

HS: In the state newspapers?

NM: All the newspapers were state newspapers.

HS: Did they talk about Jews in the papers, or was it a matter of the usual Eastern bloc blah-blah-blah about "Zionists" and "the fascist-imperialist-decadent State of Israel?"

NM: No, no, no. Relations with Israel were okay. Romania was the only socialist country that had diplomatic relations with Israel. We're talking here about *essential Romania*, a very interesting place! Of course, not so interesting if you lived there. When I left the country, I told myself, "I can't live in a place this interesting anymore." Over there you no longer knew with whom you were talking. Everything was complicated, and *much* too interesting.

So. Romania opposed the Soviet bloc, and had relations with Israel. Romania didn't participate in the 1968 invasion of Czechoslovakia, either. Romania was *l'enfant terrible*, the spoiled child, admired by the West. Our leader was received by the queen of England, by the German chancellor, by French notables. They were all in love with Romania. Of course, no one cared what was going on inside the country. They were interested in the game of international politics, and in this game Romania played an equivocal role.

Anti-Semitism was subterranean and implicit, and it also became public. The word *Jew* was used, not as a pejorative. How could it be otherwise? Officially one wasn't allowed to use words equivalent to *Yid or Kike*. A cultural weekly called *The Week,* visibly connected to Securitate[3], used to publish frequent attacks on Jews, on Jewish writers. At a certain moment, *The Week* published a list of pseudonyms. In my case there wasn't one, but Leibovici was Duda [Mulberry]; his brother, also Leibovici, was Raicu [a Romanian family name]; Legrel was Mugur [a Romanian family name meaning "Bud"]; and so on and so forth. That was the game. "What's a Jew?" asks a Romanian joke. Answer? "A Jew is a Kike that just left the room." The Yid is a Jew as long as he's in a social setting. The moment he leaves, he goes back to being a Yid for the others—which is to say,

---

3 Securitate was the Romanian secret service.

being what he is.

Once a Securitate officer visited me and asked me why I didn't leave. Hidden behind this question lay their intention to ethnically purify the country. Otherwise they had nothing against a Jewish writer's writing about Jews. "This is your little corner! Write about Jews—or, even better, leave the country and go to Palestine! Don't write about us. Don't think you are a Romanian writer, that you are Romanian. Don't delude yourself."

I considered myself a Romanian writer. I once got very angry about an anthology published in Israel in the '70s in which I appeared, among others. I was a very young writer at the time. I think I had published just one book. The title of the anthology was *Jewish Writers of the Romanian Language*. What! I am a Romanian writer! No one has the right to ask me if I am a Jew. I am a Jew—I don't deny it—but here it's a matter of something else: I am a Romanian writer because this is the language in which I write.

But if you ask me today, after 40 years, I must confess I'm somehow no longer so sure if they weren't right in the end. I'm really not sure at all.

HS: Let's return to 1986. How did daily life look back then?

NM: Rotten. My father, who was around eighty years old, had to get up early, at 5 o'clock, to stand in line for a bottle of milk, and bread. In winter people went virtually without heat. It wasn't Transnistria, but we were comparing the situation to a country-sized concentration camp. On one hand, anti-Semitism had become manifest; on the other, I used to think it wouldn't be decent to complain of anti-Semitism when the whole country found itself in such a frightful situation. I think eighty percent of Romanians would have preferred to be Jews, because they would have been able to leave the country, even if they had to put up with anti-Semitism. For this reason, then, I didn't think it would be decent to lament.

HS: Did you hear remarks about Jews when you stood in line to buy milk?

NM: There, and in the tram, and on the bus, and not only there—as happens in times of crisis. Romania didn't have a wonderful past in this regard. Ana Pauker was no longer alive; you could no longer make Hannah Rabinsohn guilty of the whole catastrophe. But rumors went around: "Maybe even Ceauşescu is Jewish," on the theory that *ceauş* means *usher* in Romanian, so maybe someone in his family had been a synagogue usher. I wrote somewhere that if you wore eyeglasses in a concentration camp there was no big difference for the other detainees. For you, however, there was a big distinction.

HS: Why?

NM: If the patrol ripped the glasses off your nose and broke them, you were not just a victim; you were ridiculous, too. You fumbled around blindly to the laughter of the gallery. There was no great difference in being a Jew in those times… but still, there were differences.

H.S: It was like being shut up in a concentration camp without glasses.

NM: It's no great joy, returning to the insolvable Jewish question over and over again.

–THE EIGHTH DIALOGUE–
The Long Goodbye

HS: How did you manage to leave Romania in 1986?

NM: I was in contact with several German writers from Bucharest. I could say Romanian writers of German language. They told me that I had received a DAAD[4] grant in Berlin—

HS: For which you hadn't even applied.

NM: Ernest Wichner, a German writer who had emigrated from Romania to the Federal Republic of Germany submitted for me, but I never received a confirmation letter.

The Germans aren't Italians. When they want to communicate something to you, they send you a letter! I know them. They have a well-organized archive with the names of the people they killed, for example. They are disciplined and organized—and that's both good and bad, as we know. Meanwhile, I received nothing. At a certain moment we decided—my wife and I—to ask for a passports for a touristic visit to Cella's sister in Washington. And for the first time in our long life, the guardians agreed that we could leave together. I don't believe this was a coincidence. I already had a sufficiently tense relationship with the authorities. I was attacked in the newspapers. My novel *The Black Envelope* had been massacred by the censors. Spies surrounded me. I suppose they wanted to get rid of me. They gave us the passports. I bought tickets to Washington via West Berlin. Back then, the tickets cost a year's salary.

We made a stopover in Berlin, and we lived for two or three days with my friend and translator the writer Paul Schuster, a passionate and honest man. I asked him the second day to ring the people at DAAD and ask them if it were true that I had received the grant. "Of course!" they answered. "We don't know what happened to Norman Manea, though!" Paul Schuster threw them

---

4 DAAD (*Deutscher Akademischer Austausch Dienst*) is the German Academic Exchange Service.

the bomb: "He's here." "He's here? Really?" They invited us to have lunch with them, and they showed us the letter that they had, of course, sent on time, but which had been returned, stamped "RECIPIENT UNKNOWN."

Explain to me, please, with your rational Western mind: Where is the logic in this whole business? They gave me the passport, but they didn't let me find out about this grant, although it was evident that after I arrived in the West I would obviously find out about it! I tried to discover the logic in this lack of logic so typical of the system. The explanation I arrived at in the end was linked to the fact that, back then, any grant would have to be approved by the first lady of the country, Comrade Elena Ceausescu, who was responsible for the party line in culture and science. The people from Securitate who oversaw correspondence knew that she would not approve a grant for a year in Berlin. She approved very selectively, and only for a few weeks. A one year grant for some character with the peculiar name *Norman*?

All this is speculation. They approved my tourist passport. Another section was responsible for official travel. Tourism here; official travel over there. It's possible that the two sections didn't inform each other. It's possible that they did know, and that they said, "Let's let him leave. He won't come back. Bye-bye." However things worked out, I got the passport.

In the period before leaving I met a colleague, a poet, on the street in Bucharest. She had just returned from Paris, and she said to me, "We're writers. We have to stay here." "That's our bad luck," I answered. "Anyhow, that was my justification for forty years. Now it's no longer valid. If you go to the cemetery, you'll find many writers. They're still here, but they can't write anymore. To write, you have to be alive. If you die, you can't write anymore. It's suicide to leave your country to live in exile, but it's a potential suicide. Staying here is certain death. Not necessarily because they'll kill us, but because we may get sick and not get to the hospital on time."

It was impossible, for example, to find a taxi. We had a close friend whose wife needed dialysis every other day. Finding a car to bring her to the hospital and back was a nightmare. Finally he found a truck driver who was transporting bricks.

HS: What happened to you then?

NM: We continued our trip to Washington. We stayed there for three weeks. Then we returned to Berlin. We had to go to the Romanian embassy to prolong the visa. Because we were in *West* Berlin, on the other side of the Wall, they couldn't refuse. I wanted to be within the law. I hadn't decided yet to remain in the West. I delayed that decision for far too long. As I already told you, separations are hard on me—from anyone and anything.

My parents had remained in Romania. My mother was gravely ill. My parents lived in a small city, and they were surviving with great difficulty. We used to send them packages with coffee and sausages, medication and cookies. Packages with food are sent to a concentration camp, not to a normal country. The year in Berlin was very pleasant on one hand. I felt stimulated on account of the language, the atmosphere. On the other hand it was a year full of turmoil because of the radical decisions we would have to make.

HS: Where did you stay in Berlin?

NM: In the neighborhood of Rathenau Square, on a small street, Storkwinkel, in a building for DAAD grantees. I recall I was invited to visit several apartments. I was to choose one that I liked. I wasn't an American or Canadian grantee, wasn't used to choosing, so I said, "Wonderful! Perfect! Full of light!" to the first apartment that was shown me. I didn't want to even see another apartment that might be better, more elegant.

That year was full of questions. Every day we talked about what we should do. My mother was desperate. She understood I would not return. It was a tense, complicated year, but in 1987 I also experienced the joy of publishing my first book in German: *Robot Biography and Other Stories*, at Steidl Verlag. The book was received surprisingly well. I hadn't expected this rapid change of situation.

HS: Did you write anything during that period?

NM: No. It was a very tense year. I wasn't in any shape to write. I kept reading newspapers and magazines, all the magazines. I was famished for information, which I couldn't previously get. That year was therefore pleasant, complicated and tense. Many people advised me to seek political asylum. I didn't want to. I didn't know what I should do. I was afraid of the fact that my folks might be harassed. I didn't want to make their situation more complicated than it was. I looked—and this is my typical hesitation when facing an uncertain future—I looked for a delay of any clear, firm, definitive decision. I was hoping that our great leader would die, finally—the only finale we could imagine—the biological resolution. I wanted to spend a year or two in the West. Then everything would change for the better. After that, then we'd see.

When my grant ended—that was in December 1987—DAAD extended it for me for another three months. I looked for another grant during that time. I didn't succeed. We had some money we'd saved during the year we spent in Berlin. We left for a month in Paris. I would have liked to remain in Paris.

HS: Time and again, all Romanians in exile make it to Paris.

NM: Because it seems simpler in terms of their habits, life-style, and language. I was intimidated, though, by the overly large Romanian exile community in Paris. Again, it was suggested to me that I seek political asylum. I didn't want it. Then I received the Fulbright scholarship to the Catholic University in Washington.

HS: Had you applied for this grant?

NM: It was suggested that I make a request, and then yes, I applied. This is again an excessively bizarre story for anyone who doesn't understand anything of the all too interesting and codified world of the East.

Cella has a sister in Washington. Her husband used to work for USIA, the United States Information Agency, an institution for cultural exchange between the United States and the rest of the world. It no longer exists. Back then it took care of grants, among other things, and my brother-in-law knew that for seven years Romanians hadn't participated in the Fulbright scholarships for Romania.

HS: What does that mean?

NM: That Romanians hadn't honored this governmental exchange of scholarships; they hadn't sent even one Fulbright holder to America—for seven years! American scholars came to Romania, but not one Romanian counterpart made it to America. Consequently there were discussions about whether it might not be better to give the Fulbright scholarships to Hungary. This is what the American grant officer for Romania told me when I arrived in Washington. A very gracious American, very intelligent, he had written his dissertation on the history of the Romanians, spoke excellent Romanian, knew Romanian jokes—and it was he who warned his colleagues that Hungary was (and has remained) Romania's historic enemy, for which reason the United States could not allow itself this kind of mistake. He proposed finding Romanian intellectuals living outside Romania. The foundation would write a letter to the government of Romania that would inform the government it would offer the scholarships to some of these people. Experience kept showing that the government of Romania would respond neither yea nor nay; the Americans would consider the Romanian silence tacit acceptance.

That's how I received the Fulbright scholarship to the Catholic University in Washington.

–THE NINTH DIALOGUE–
On Israel

HS: Why, as a former member of the Betar organization, didn't you immigrate to Israel instead? You had family there, after all.

NM: Not only family, but also friends. I might have emigrated legally—not with a suitcase, as happened in fact, but with 70 kilograms of personal goods. That's not a remarkable weight for a human life, but it also doesn't fit in a single suitcase. Not only former members of the Betar organization and members of opposed, left-leaning, Zionist organizations took refuge in Israel. There were communist refugees, social democrats, socialists—and not just rank and file members, but also leaders of these parties.

One of my friends who left Romania and established himself in Israel was Leon Volovici, the literary historian. At first he worked for *Yad Vashem*[5]; now he's at the Hebrew University in Jerusalem. Volovici wrote me, "If you want to be a Jew, go to Israel. If you want to be a writer, don't go to Israel."

HS: Why?

NM: Because as a Romanian writer in Israel, you'd lose yourself completely in a tiny ghetto. Things stand differently today. Today there is even a Romanian television channel. But back then Romanians amounted to just a minuscule cultural ghetto. Completely different from the Russian community.

HS: Do you really need a community to be a writer?

NM: No, but if you're a Romanian writer in Tel Aviv, what do you do?

HS: You write your books, and in the evening you savor the street promenade.

NM: And the manuscripts? Do you leave them to your widow and

---

5 The Holocaust Martyrs' and Heroes' Remembrance Authority

children in your will? Or maybe to the State of Israel?

HS: What would really have been different in Tel Aviv, compared to Paris—or to Bard College in New York?

NM: If you live in Paris you benefit from the goods and evils of a great metropolis with a fabulous cultural history, and you may even succeed in publishing something there. At Bard College you learn something about academic America, and maybe you even try to publish something. In Israel, my friend Leon Volovici didn't see even the smallest possibility back then—and he was right—that a Jewish writer of Romanian origin would be translated into Hebrew. Israel doesn't want us too much. Not even when you have the advantage of living in Paris.

HS: Because Israelis have this arrogant attitude: *Io zrichim et se*—we don't need this.

NM: They give the Jerusalem Prize to many writers of value, but rarely to a Jewish writer. And when they do give it, then they give it to a Jewish writer who isn't too Jewish: Susan Sontag, for example. It's a decision, I think, of a leftist literary group over there. This year, 2009, twenty years since the fall of Communism, do you think the Jerusalem Prize could have been given to an East European writer of Jewish origin—for example Imre Kertész, or Ivan Klima, or Györge Konrád, or Péter Nádas, or Wolf Biermann? No, the prize was conferred on Haruki Murakami. I have absolutely nothing against Murakami, but why don't they give the Jerusalem Prize to a non-Jewish writer from Eastern Europe, on this occasion at least? We're only celebrating the fall of the Berlin Wall this year, and this is very important. Why wasn't the prize given to Kadare, or Wyborska, or to one of the Russians, who would have deserved it the same as all the others I've named?

You know what they say: "It takes two to tango." That's how the saying goes in America. I danced the solitary tango for long enough in Romania. But in Israel I would have danced alone too.

HS: Did you know Israel, in fact?

NM: My first trip abroad was to Israel. I was then young and innocent; I was forty years old. To make a first trip abroad at forty years of age seems original to you, I suspect.

HS: Did you like Israel?

NM: Yes. I was very impressed by Israel. There I experienced a shock: Everyone is Jewish! The policeman is Jewish and the prostitute is Jewish.

I liked the country, and the atmosphere. I liked the transformation I saw in members of my family, people who had left Romania and become Israelis. They wouldn't have had an enviable life in Romania—in any case, not the life that they were living in Israel. This is not to suggest that they all became the prime minister, or rich, in Israel. No, they had an ordinary life, but this ordinary life was several classes above the one they'd lived in Romania.

The encounter with Israel aroused powerful sentiments, too, because it was my first visit to a free country. I remember the first night. I arrived in the afternoon, and a cousin of mine with whom I had been together in the camp, and then in Socialist Romania, hosted us at her home in Jerusalem. I went to the Wailing Wall. That was very powerful, emotionally. Then, at night, at her place, I found several books on a shelf. In French I read the memoir written by the widow of the poet Peretz Markisch, the Jewish poet who was born in 1895 in Volhynia and killed on the night of August twelfth to thirteenth, 1952, together with approximately thirty other Jews, in Lubianka prison, with a bullet to the back of the neck on the order of Joseph Stalin. I read all night. I found out about many odd things. I knew that he had been killed, but I didn't know the whole story. And it's happened to me this way with many other things.

I was thinking then—and I still believe this—that the foundation of the State of Israel is one of the most important events of the twentieth century.

HS: The country didn't seem foreign to you?

NM: But yes, of course. For a Jew from Central Europe, Jerusalem isn't the most orderly, elegant, or clean city, but what fascination it produces! Jerusalem remains a very special place for me, a really wonderful city with a unique atmosphere, and I regret that almost exclusively pious people live there now. I loved the madness of the country and the people. Of course, it's more

Oriental than I would like, personally, but it is as it is, and it is extraordinary.

HS: What thoughts and feelings does Israel arouse in you today?

NM: Israel has become a country beleaguered, not only by Arab neighbors but by the whole world. Since the Palestinian problem has become so acute for the international left, which is ready to forget that it was impossible to conclude a peace with the Arabs for decades, the Palestinians are considered an oppressed people that lives under occupation and in exile, and it is therefore possible to diffuse the most flimflamming theories and false scenarios today, all of them betraying history and current reality, just as it is now finally permissible say of the Holocaust everything that couldn't be said fifty years ago—even that it, too, is a Zionist invention, as Mahmoud Ahmadinejad said in Teheran, he himself being ready to provoke a new Holocaust at any time, and a more convincing one than the one before.

A rational question may be posed as well: Why did no European state cede the Jews a bit of land if the guilt for the Holocaust is European? In *The Hooligan's Return* there is an amusing passage in which I imagine that Israel might have been founded in Bavaria, ceded to the Jews by the Germans as compensation for the Holocaust.

Several years ago I gave a public lecture in Italy. A middle-aged lady addressed me as follows: "I have read your book. It's very moving. I understand that you have passed through very difficult situations, and so I ask you, doesn't the suffering of other people, the Palestinians for example, move you, too?" "But yes, of course," I answered. "Any suffering moves me, including the suffering of the Palestinians. Why would such suffering leave me indifferent?" "Okay," my interlocutor went on. "Then tell me: Why did the Jews return to Palestine? In this way, they created an enormous problem, which isn't resolved even after sixty years." My answer to her was, "I can't respond in the name of the Jews, and there isn't time to enter into all the details of historic motivations. It's a complicated matter. The history of the Jews, and of Zionism, would have to be studied. But I would rather respond to the question with a question, as the Jews often do. At the end of the Second World War, would Italy have given up Tuscany to host the State of Israel? You, as an Italian, would you have agreed to this solution?" She fell silent. "I, as a Romanian, can assure you that Romania wouldn't have given the Jews so much as a province, not even a city."

My interlocutor wasn't discouraged. "But Canada?" she asked. I gave in without giving in. "We'll have to invite the Canadian ambassador to respond to that question."

HS: Have you read Michael Chabon's wonderful novel *The Yiddish Policemen's Union*? He imagines that the Arabs had already defeated the Zionists in 1948. The Americans let the surviving Jews colonize Alaska, but this right is theirs for only sixty years.

NM: I don't know if the author consulted with Sarah Palin, but I can say with certainty that if Israel disappears off the map, the Near East will become perfect, instantly. The Sunnis will kiss the Shiites; the Kurds, Bedouins, and Christians will all love each other. Finally it will be as in Paradise. The Jews are the only problem in the Near East. Immediately after they disappear, the Arabs will forget their wars, their murders, the hatred they bear each other, the fanaticism with which they judge the "infidels" of all races and beliefs. If this will happen in my lifetime, I don't know.

–THE TENTH DIALOGUE–
Pedestrian in America

HS: Let's return to the other crazy country: America. You arrived here in 1988 on a Fulbright scholarship. You had a student visa. For how long?

NM: For a year. I arrived in March, and the scholarship went on until the end of the year. Then it was extended for another four months.

HS: Until that moment, had you decided to stay or go back to Romania?

NM: No. I had made absolutely no decision. I was as disoriented as before. My mother had died in July 1988, several months after I arrived here, and without consulting me my father had made a request to immigrate to Israel.

HS: Where were you in America? In Washington?

NM: Yes.

HS: You had lived one year in Washington and you still didn't know what to do.

NM: Yes. As you see, I'm not drawing myself a very flattering portrait.

HS: What determined you to stay here, in the end? Was it the circumstance that your mother had died and your father was in Israel?

NM: This contributed to my decision, of course, but it wasn't the main reason. The final reason—because I am very sluggish about anything regarding separation—was post-'89 Romania.

HS: Of what were you afraid?

NM: Of everything. Even though I was thinking that I could never adapt here. I spoke about this with Philip Roth.

HS: How did you meet him?

NM: I wrote to him from Berlin. He was living in London then. I wrote to him because he was publishing a series of books back then, *Writers from the Other Europe: Milan Kundera, Bruno Schulz*.... He was an American that knew something, at least, about Eastern Europe, and I wrote to him proposing an anthology of contemporary Romanian prose, published in Romania. From Berlin, I sketched out my dilemma for him. Roth replied in a very friendly way. He pointed out several people in Paris for me, and he concluded with a kind of invitation: "If you get to America eventually, call me." My plans were European back then, but when I arrived in America, we met. And at a certain moment during our discussion, he asked me, "What do you expect here? What do you want?" I told him, "A hole. A hole to hide myself in. That's all I want." And he smiled. "In America there are a lot of things that you can't even imagine now, but a hole to hide yourself in you will not find." This may help you to understand how I felt back then. Yes, I was afraid of America. I kept thinking that my temperament, my sensibility, my solitary nature wouldn't let me make it in this country.

HS: I'm surprised. In the end it's remarkable that here, in America, you're left in peace. You can roam the street with a paper bag on your head or never leave your house for a year at a time; no one will take you amiss, provided you pay your bills and debts on time.

NM: If I were a vegetable seller, my store would have gone into bankruptcy. If I were a grocery clerk it would have been the same. And on top of that, I don't know how to drive a car, so I couldn't have worked as a cabbie, either.

HS: It's funny, I don't know how to drive a car either.

NM: But you're a correspondent for *Die Welt*. I wasn't a correspondent for an important Romanian review; I was a nobody. I felt terribly estranged from this landscape, from this community, even from American Jews, who were a completely new species for me.

HS: In what sense?

NM: In all senses, if we think of my past. Jews who go to the gym regularly, Jews who enjoy nature; optimistic Jews! These aren't my Jews.

That aside, I had the big linguistic problem too. When I arrived I didn't speak English at all. I didn't understand what was being said in the subway. I was a deaf-mute in a foreign world.

Very difficult, especially for a writer, who was suddenly deprived of what was essential for him: his language. But I no longer have the right to complain. Gradually and eventually, things took a positive turn. If I think retrospectively, I was lucky, without any contribution on my part to the planning of this luck—in which I didn't even believe. It is much better now that I am here than in any of the other places where I would have liked to remain, either Germany (I liked Berlin back then, and I like it very much now too) or Paris.

HS: Where were you when you heard the news that Ceaușescu had been shot?

NM: I was in New York. I was living—and my wife with me—in an unpleasant little room in a miserable place on 48th Street and Eighth Avenue. Back then prostitutes and drug dealers hung out there all the time. In every man on the street I saw a delinquent who could kill me any second if he were in a bad mood.

HS: You consequently ascertained that everything communist propaganda affirmed about the Occident and America had all just proved true, and that it wasn't the least exaggerated.

NM: When I was in Berlin I received a letter from a friend. "Now you'll see," he wrote, "everything the communists say about capitalism is true, and everything the capitalists say about communism is likewise true. This won't help you see your life in a very optimistic way."

HS: Did you write anything in that period?

NM: In the summer of 1989 I was invited to Bard College. I remember the date well: July 9, 1989, Cella's birthday. Leon Botstein, the president of the college, had read my books in German. I received the key to our house on campus, and I was very happy. That summer I wrote a novella called *The Raincoat* (*Trenciul*). In September I began to teach at Bard College.

We were still living in our dilapidated hotel in New York. At the end of November the events in Romania began. All of Europe was on the move. There was chaos and tension in Timişoara and Bucharest, the tense expectation of what would come next. I spoke on American television during those disturbed days, before and after the dictator's disappearance. The news that he was killed, the images, reached me in my hotel room. I remember exactly. I was very disturbed. The procedure for liquidating the despot shocked me.

HS: Weren't you happy that the monster was finally dead?

NM: I was disgusted and worried because of the way things happened. A typical Stalinist procedure. I had no reason to love that stuttering and syntax-wrecking illiterate. I despised him. Even in 1968—Ceauşescu's moment of grace from a political point of view, when he made a pronouncement against the invasion of Czechoslovakia from the balcony of Central Committee headquarters—even then, when some people were floating in seventh heaven, I wasn't floating. I didn't trust him from the very beginning.

But the way he was treated gave me a moment of nausea, of repulsion, disorientation. I was frightened of the way this trial had been staged: a summary trial, directed by new manipulators. I had hoped there would be a real trial of dictatorship, communism, and those forty years. A trial of Securitate, and even of the opportunism in the country. Ceauşescu wasn't the only guilty party, even if his guilt couldn't be easily forgotten. Some later maintained that his trial had to take place very quickly because it wasn't known how the situation would evolve. I remember after I saw the news I took a long walk, and I felt distressed and bitter. Although after that intellectuals and writers—among whom there were some I knew and admired—took part in the government, this was not at all a good moment.

I was ready to return to Romania, though. I was talking to friends who were in exile as well, and I was telling them, "Now we ought to return. The reason we left no longer exists. We can hope again."

My friends proved more realistic than I. They wanted us to wait, to see first of all what was going on. And what happened soon was that the political atmosphere in the country, and the intellectual debates, gave me the sensation that many intellectuals were oriented toward 1938, not toward 2000. The great models of the past returned, haloed with new glory, and they weren't my models.

HS: In other words, the story soon turned disgusting and nationalist.

NM: Very soon. And some of the intellectuals who had entered politics participated in this game. I don't know if they even believed in the new/old political orientation, if they liked this form of primary nationalism and anti-communism, or if they were only participating to maintain their positions. Then, too, the way the old *nomenklatura* had found to arrange itself in these new conditions was very repulsive.

HS: This return to nationalism contains a certain dose of historical irony, doesn't it? In the end, even the Ceauşescu regime was nationalist.

NM: In its last decade of existence, the regime had renounced internationalism and replaced it with nationalism.

HS: It was consequently a form of national socialism.

NM: Or national communism. It was interesting, sometimes astonishing. If you had gone into a bookstore in Bucharest and asked for the works of Karl Marx, you would have been looked at like an idiot, or a mental case, or a provocateur. It was impossible to imagine that someone would do something like that. Beyond that, Marx wasn't to be found anywhere. But you could find the complete works—in twenty or thirty volumes—of our great leader. That was Romania! It was a façade of Byzantine socialism. We can avail ourselves today, as well, of that good characterization, thanks to a Romanian-Jewish communist who was locked up and condemned to death while he devoted himself to the Party as if it were a drug.

HS: Under the fascists.

NM: No, under the communists. Belu Zilber he was called. Zilber said of Romanian Communism that it was a mixture of Stalin and Caragiale. Ion Luca Caragiale was and is the most important Romanian satiric writer.

–The Eleventh Dialogue–
The Rabbi

HS: Tell me, please, how did you get to be at Bard College?

NM: I had a recommendation from Mary McCarthy. She was teaching at Bard then, and happily I was able to talk with her in French. Then, too, I've told you that I had met Philip Roth. He had told me that Bard College might a possibility for me because the college was offering a kind of grant for intellectuals who could not express themselves freely in their own country. He asked me if some book of mine had appeared in English or German. I had a book in German, and Leon Botstein, the president of the college, read German. Philip asked me to send Leon the book. It was the volume that had appeared at Steidl: *Robot Biography and Other Stories*. Botstein read it, he was enthusiastic, and invited me to hold two seminars at Bard. For me it was a debut. I had never taught, and now I had to do it in a foreign country and a foreign language.

I was invited to Bard. I shook hands with the president, and I thought to myself, like a good Balkanic-Byzantine Romanian, that the problem was solved. But Botstein said, "No, Norman. As you may know, you're living in a democracy now, so you have to appear before a committee." I had already told him when he raised the question of my teaching that I had a not at all minor difficulty: "I don't speak English very well." His answer was, "Einstein didn't know English either." "Except that I'm not Einstein," the Romanian replied. "I don't teach mathematics and physics. I'll be discussing books with the students. I have to be able to speak with them." "Hey, it'll come," Botstein replied.

HS: But at that time you knew some English.

NM: In the year we spent in Washington, we both—Cella and I— attended a course for immigrants along with some elderly Chinese ladies, beautiful girls from Brazil, and nomads from all over the world—Iran, Russia, what have you. It was an introductory course that lasted three months. That's all I did in an official way. The rest I learned on my own, in daily life: from newspapers, television, discussion, lectures, and so forth.

In this way I arrived in front of the committee made up of six people who were teaching at Bard—

HS: Really? You went into a room and there were these six people seated at a table and they questioned you?

NM: Yes. They asked me what I did in Romania, what my books are about, what I might do at Bard College. In every academic institution there are, as you know, groups, intrigues, and battles. And I didn't know the sides in the conflict. I didn't know what the front line was. Not at all. The only sure thing was that I had been proposed by the president. There were the president's enemies there too, of course, but I didn't know them; I didn't know the games in the wings of the stage.

At the end, one professor put to me the following question: "It is true that we have this grant, but we have to be very careful about whom we give to, and for what reasons. My question to you is as follows: What will happen if you go back to Romania?" I answered hesitantly. "I don't know. Maybe you expect I will tell you that they will kill me or throw me in prison... but I don't know. Maybe nothing will happen to me. Maybe a traffic accident will take place in the street, maybe I'll go to the hospital, maybe it will go well for me...."

After this interview I hadn't the least bit of news from Bard College. Not a sign, for a very long time.

HS: How long?

NM: For a month and a half or more. And I thought, "That was it. I failed." I stayed in my deluxe hotel in New York on the street with prostitutes and drug dealers. It was a lot of fun. Then I was called by the people from Bard. "We would like you to come another time and talk with us some more. There were some discussion here, and the administration believes that a second meeting is necessary." Good. So I went to Bard College again. I met with the dean—not with the president—and the dean said to me, "You will have eight interviews now, each for half an hour, with eight different professors. Then you'll come back to me."

Eight interviews! I flung myself headfirst into this adventure. The first interview was with a Belgian professor. I was very glad that she was Belgian; I could speak French with her. I didn't know what the under-workings were this time, either. She asked me, "What will you teach here?" "Ah, I don't know," I babbled. "I could hold a seminar about the Holocaust, for example." "So it will be the literature of the Holocaust. What authors are you thinking of?" I enumerated—Appelfeld, Primo Levi, and so on. Then she figured she better put the dot on the letter *i*: "*I* teach the literature of the Holocaust here."

HS: So you gave the wrong answer.

NM: Yes. I said, "I'm sorry. That's what you asked me." I was like August the Fool, who understood his stupidity. Then other interviews followed. In the end I returned to the dean. I was given to understand that this time everything had been a quasi-formality. For me, though, it was very stressful to go through eight interviews with eight people whom I was seeing for the first time and to answer all kinds of questions. The dean pronounced the verdict: "Norman, we're hiring you. We're giving you the grant. It's not too big, but you'll also receive a house here at Bard. You'll teach two seminars. The grant is for a year. Would you like to go back to the station now?" "Yes," I said. "Okay, a student is waiting for you with a car." Happy as I was, I went to the car. The girl was already at the wheel, a Brazilian student. She asked me if I wanted to go to the station. Sure. "But we have to wait for the rabbi," she said. "For the rabbi? Okay." After about ten minutes, the rabbi came along: a young woman in jeans, with a bag over her shoulder. She wasn't the kind of East-European rabbi I used to know. She was an American rabbi, and I an old East-European Jew. We went to the station together. The train was two hours delayed. It was coming from Toronto. So I had a discussion with the *rebbetzin*.

She had a lot of thick books with her: the *Kabbalah*, the *Talmud*, things of that kind. I asked her, "When did you decide to become a rabbi, and why?" "I felt the need for connection with the community," she said. "Community! I come from a communist society, and I can't hear the word *community* anymore. It became unbearable for me. I don't want to have anything to do with the community, no matter which community we're talking about." The young woman looked at me, surprised, even shocked. Then I asked her about her family. "Are your parents still living? Are you close?" "They divorced." "Aha. How old were you when your parents divorced?" "I was 13." "And how was it?" "It was the biggest shock of my life." "Do you have other brothers or sisters?"

"Yes, I have a sister in California." "And what is she doing there?" "She's raising horses." "Seriously? She raises horses and you are a rabbi? How do you reconcile the two occupations?" "Well, my sister is a Buddhist." "Ah, she's Buddhist?"

This was the lesson I learned as I returned from Bard to New York. I understood where I was: in another world. Any preconception was superfluous; any search for coherence was in vain.

–THE TWELFTH DIALOGUE–
The Right to Stupidity

HS: You once said that America is a good hotel.

NM: And I still think so. And it seems very important to me that it be so. I like that the government here is called "the Administration." An administration that deals with current affairs. If it's efficient, that's all right; if it's not efficient, we vote another one in. There are no identity cards. The state has no right to know where I live, what I think, how patriotic I am. Right from the start, all these things stuck me as wonderful.

I like this country's incoherence. I believe that if it were coherent, as George W. Bush hoped and dreamed, it would be a catastrophe.

HS: What do you mean by that?

NM: I hope that America will never be a perfectly homogenous construction, an entity you can easily define. It's hard to reduce America to a common denominator. I've kept thinking about this. When you think that you've finally found an essential defining characteristic, be it good or bad, and you say. "This is it! This is America!" That's when you realize, after some reflection—

HS: —that the opposite of this quality is equally valid.

NM: Exactly. And this is precisely what I like: the incoherence.

HS: For example, America is a country with mostly religious inhabitants, in which atheistic books are frequently bestsellers.

NM: Not only that; one of the most important industrial branches of this religious country is the porn industry. America declared itself a pragmatic country from the very beginning. It's a country based on a religious premise, but one that separates church and state. How can you be pragmatic and religious at the same time? To be pragmatic means integrating yourself in daily life, elbowing your way forward; to be religious means that you have principles that you can't abandon—ever. There is a contradiction here, and there are many contradictions in America. You find some of everything here—charity, fraternity, demagogy, cordiality, innocence, tolerance, greed, stupidity—everything a free man can offer. I once wrote an essay about the right to stupidity. It seemed to me something out of the ordinary.

HS: How so?

NM: In our countries, especially in Eastern Europe, it is shameful to be stupid, to be considered stupid. If you're stupid, people tell you so, and you have to stand in a corner, ashamed. In the United States, people say colossally stupid things, which are accepted as possible variants of thought, expressions of individuality.

Maybe that's exaggerated, but in the right to stupidity I still recognize a fundamental human right. Be stupid! Why not? Are those who tell a person one hundred times that he's an idiot—as we hear someone or other apostrophized in Romania every five minutes—are the ones who insult this way really so intelligent and enlightened? The simple man on the street often seems stupid, but he isn't; he has healthy common sense. In America I came face to face with the intellectual's more modest position. I had to depart from the elitist conception, and to understand that our position as intellectuals isn't set apart.

This doesn't mean that I am never frustrated by the anti-intellectualism of this country. In America there are many important writers and poets. Not one of them was interviewed on television about the war in Iraq. How are we doing in Afghanistan? How do you see our situation? No. Never! The writers are off somewhere in isolated houses in the woods or at the ocean, in their writing rooms, and they are shown a tepid respect. In this trivial democracy—for that's what America is: a popular, trivial democracy—who is the hero? The basketball player. The movie star. The rich banker. We're looking at another kind of elitism, an anti-intellectual one, based on social success.

HS: May I defend American anti-intellectualism a bit?

NM: Of course you may. And you'll see right away that I approve.

HS: Intellectuals are often completely out of joint, from a political point of view. They support bloody dictatorships. In any case, they aren't smarter than other people from a political point of view. Why should public opinion listen patiently to their opinions?

NM: Because they too are part of public opinion. They aren't more out of joint than the masses, with their volatile, easily manipulated enthusiasms. Otherwise you are perfectly right. I only told you that I accept my position in America. Still, I have moments of frustration from time to time, for, willy-nilly, I am one of them, the intellectuals, too. To give you an example, though, the following thing happens: I fly to Europe, arrive at Frankfurt, buy *Frankfurter Allgemeine Zeitung*. There I see an article about how a poet in Bremen has reached 60 years of age, so they're celebrating his birthday. Which deserves an article! Here the poet Richard Eberhart died not long ago—an important American poet—at the age of one hundred and one, and that meant nothing so far as American public opinion goes.

HS: Since you've mentioned it, what bothers you most in America?

NM: When I arrived in America I watched the television, and on the news I learned that in Washington, several streets away from where I was staying, a dog had been run over by a car. The dog's owners were destroyed. They were sobbing out loud. And the neighbors came to console them. Nice, very good, lovely. But was this the most important news of the day? A dog was run over by a car; that was the day's repeated news item. I've spent a lot of time watching these American news stories, so many of them provincial, infantile, self-sufficient, and highly oriented toward the immediately domestic, and I've thought, "Maybe it should be like this. Maybe it's more human. But changing the channel to the BBC or to the French news, you see that other things of interest are happening in the world, and they are not minor.

HS: To put it this way, while a dog was run over by a car in Washington, a nuclear war nearly broke out between India and Pakistan.

NM: Exactly. What irritates me is this provincialism of a very great country, its isolation, its "self-sufficiency."

HS: America behaves as if it were an island.

NM: It is as isolated as an island, and provincial at the same time, although it is a superpower. Very proud, Americans often affirm that they are the first in whichever or whatever discipline, and they have no idea at all who's the second or third, or what or how the others are, the ones who might be—who knows?—in fact the first. Smacking of sports or the military, this inflamed and infantile language is applied even to the outcome of jury trial. The finale of the process is seen as a competition, as a boxing match between the prosecutor and the defense attorney. The victor is in seventh heaven; the other guy can lose his job tomorrow. I could never understand this. For me a trial at law is something else completely.

HS: Is Capitalism guilty of all these things?

NM: I don't really see an alternative. I've just lived too long under Socialism. But it could be that some legislative touch ups are needed, even if that would mean a slow-down in the rhythm of development. Naturally, I am for a free society, for competition, for a free market, but the social system in America is very prejudiced by stunning economic contrasts. At a certain moment I asked Philip Roth if he might name a principle, a basis on which this country is founded. He answered that the fathers of the country had wanted to promote freedom and support fierce competition, or at least to accept it. In their opinion this competition was the engine of social progress, but the rule was that at the end the winner should not let the loser fall too low. That would damage the health of the society. In reality, though, competition has gotten tougher and tougher, fiercer and fiercer, and the winner no longer cares about the loser at all.

In Romania I once met with a friend who had been a grantee in America for full year. I asked him, "Tell me one thing—a single thing—that specially impressed you in America." "The situation of the ugly woman," he answered. "The ugly woman doesn't feel ugly. It's not like in Europe. She's treated as a woman, as a normal human being. Of course, people know that she isn't beautiful, but that's something they ignore."

HS: Is this really so?

NM: I don't know.

HS: And what would be, in your opinion, the singular feature that makes America so special?

NM: One would be simplification. This is the American genius: simplification. It goes hand in hand with American pragmatism. The temptation to simplify has good consequences, but some deplorable ones, too.

HS: What American phrase do you find particularly frightening?

NM: "Don't take it personally." It's a slogan you very often hear. "You're fired. Don't take it personally." How could you not take it personally? Even if it's a matter of a situation beyond personality, in the end that's what it really is: a personal matter.

HS: And what seems unusually good about America?

NM: Freedom of expression, of movement. If tomorrow my wife exasperates me and I go out of the house to buy myself a newspaper, I can disappear for twenty years. In Germany, as you know, I have to register with the police if I move from one street to the other. I like the diversity of this country. I like that it's a country of exiles. You come across exile frequently, and it is accepted.

HS: Meanwhile, you have an American passport. Have you become an American in your soul as well?

NM: Last spring I was in Romania. It seemed to me I noticed a change: I received two honorary degrees, and the President of Romania awarded me the Order of Cultural Merit.
How did this come about? After a Romanian television reporter interviewed me several years ago, it was broadcast on Romanian radio and Romanian television. Perhaps this even came about at the suggestion of that lady who interviewed me: I was alerted by my young supporter that I would receive the highest presidential distinction. Things moved very slowly, as happens in

Romania, and in the end it was no longer a matter of my receiving the highest order.

My Romanian friends advised me to refuse the distinction. They were saying, "They burned you in the public square. The jackasses should compensate you with the highest cultural order." My American friends gave me the opposite advice: "Be *gracious*." The awarding of the prize and the official dinner took place at the residence of the Romanian ambassador to the United Nations. Philip Roth and Orhan Pamuk accompanied me as bodyguards.

I didn't want to travel to Romania alone for the university honors in 2008, either. In the end, my friend Antonio Tabucchi also received the title of DHS from the University of Bucharest, and the dilemma was solved. This time I no longer refused a single interview. It was tiring, but people behaved well with me. It was comforting and encouraging particularly that the young generation was interested in my presence, not just the cultural or literary *establishment*.

When, several years ago, a Romanian journalist asked me why I don't visit the country, I answered, "Because I'm not yet indifferent." In time I have become more indifferent, thank God. And when I left Romania in 2008 after my latest visit, I understood more clearly that...

HS: It had ended.

NM: ...it was over. And when I returned to America, did I really feel that my place was there, in fact? Yes, but as in a hotel.

–THE THIRTEENTH DIALOGUE–
The Scandal

HS: Let's return to your career. Your American grant kept being extended for as much as a year. Then you received a MacArthur Fellowship for talented individuals who have shown extraordinary originality and dedication in their creative pursuits, which meant a lot of money for an immigrant. And now you have been a professor here at Bard for twenty years.

NM: With money from the MacArthur grant I made a down payment on an apartment in Manhattan. That was a very happy moment. Finally we had the key to our own home. There was the promise of a kind of stability. I had a job.

HS: In fact, your story corresponds outright to the mythological scheme of American success: An immigrant from Eastern Europe arrives without knowing the language, without money, without social connections—with the exception of Philip Roth—and succeeds here, across the ocean.

NM: No, it wasn't only Philip Roth. It was the international Jewish conspiracy! You understand? This is the main reason for the tensions with Romania. How did this guy wind up suddenly successful? There are so many Romanians in Paris and New York who failed, people who were engineers or writers before and are now driving cabs. So how did this guy succeed? In Bucharest he was so timid, so solitary. He wrote several complicated books that, of course, weren't well tolerated by the system. He had problems, but who didn't have problems. So, how? The Jews are in the middle of this! This is how they always are. They help each other. They supported him, and they helped him to make a name in this country. My Jewish wife is laughing now somewhere in the background. She thinks I'm making a joke. In fact, I'm just describing reality—Romanian reality.

In any case, my story doesn't correspond perfectly with the scheme you describe, and specifically because I don't perfectly illustrate the cliché of the survivor. (In America, the Holocaust survivor is sometimes seen as a great achiever, an important banker, a rich man, a guy who's "arrived," not a guy who seems worried and unsure of himself.) I don't see myself fitting perfectly in this scheme. Even if my current situation is as you describe it, I am still not that heroic, vital champion who leaves any confrontation as the victor. You already know me a bit, so you'll understand what I mean. And for that reason, the shock was so much the greater for those who knew me in Romania: "Why him? *We* know 'why him' precisely. We know the reason." This is one of the stimulants of tension with Romania, but there are others as well.

HS: In this context we should recall the fact that in 1991 you were in the center of a scandal. At that time *The New Republic* published an article of yours about Mircea Eliade. I read it last night, and I was surprised how mild the article is. How did everything come about?

NM: Leon Wieseltier, the literary editor of *The New Republic*, asked me to write a review of the last volume of Mircea Eliade's autobiography. I was very reticent. I knew what times I was living in, and I hadn't forgotten the anti-Semitic attacks aimed against me in the official Romanian press during the '80s. But in the end I wrote this review.

HS: A small question: When did Mircea Eliade leave Romania, in fact?

NM: During the war he was a diplomat, first in London, then—when Romania allied itself with Germany and diplomatic relations with England were no longer possible—in Lisbon. He wrote a book about António de Oliveira Salazar, the Portuguese dictator, whom he admired very much and whom he intended to propose as a model for our own dictator, Ion Antonescu. He also kept an intimate journal that was published in Romania just recently. The introduction to the Romanian edition of this journal is almost longer than the journal itself. Eliade describes his despair that Germany will lose the war. He had other motives for unhappiness as well—his wife had died; he was alone—but his big problem, nevertheless, was that the situation on the front was evolving in a direction that he didn't like. After the war he left Lisbon and went to Paris.

HS: Then he hid his past. He immigrated to America and became a famous philosopher of religion in Chicago. Could his books be bought in Ceauşescu's Romania?

NM: The communists considered him a Legionnaire, a fascist, but in the last, nationalistic stage of the regime they began to publish several of his books, and they even tried to bring him back to the country, at least for a visit, to serve the image of the Leader. It would have been a great victory to bring a VIP, a notable personality with Western recognition, back to the country. He was ready to act on this invitation, but several friends persuaded him to give it up.

HS: Mircea Eliade was a professor who wrote intricate books about remote themes.

NM: Look, you call yourself Hannes Stein! You are talking about a great cultural personality of the Romanians—an icon! Take heed!

HS: When you published the article in *The New Republic* in 1991, how may people in Romania knew Eliade's books?

NM: Do you think that all the people who talk about Jesus have read his teachings? There are names that transcend this earthly plane and become legend, symbols, or cliché. Today Eliade is one of the most important names in Romanian culture, for two reasons: First of all, he left a very rich body of work—novels, stories, scientific treatises. In the second place, he was recognized and eulogized in the West. And it's certain that he isn't Norman Manea, who has, on top of everything, another secret first name in a biblical language: Noah. Mircea Eliade is Mircea Eliade, a product of Romanian genius. The fact that I did not refer to his work in my article—that I did not even touch on it or critique it—does not count.

HS: The fact that Mircea Eliade was a fascist—I'm using this word as a specialized term, not as a swear word—was this known in Romania 1991?

NM: I don't think that the majority of Romanians knew. The older generation certainly knew—his contemporaries—and there were also people who kept up to date with the cultural debates of the years that followed. Then, think where my article appeared: in *The New Republic*, not in *The New York Times*, not in *The Washington Post*. *The New Republic* is a magazine that was appearing weekly back then—

HS: A liberal, intellectually pretentious publication that was being read, so to speak, by professors from Bard College who voted for Barack Obama.

NM: No, not necessarily. *The New Republic* is a very good cultural publication, liberal, but no longer to the left. In Romania, my article was considered a huge bomb, detonated by a Romanian Jew who defamed Mircea Eliade. Here in America the reactions were completely different. I received a very harsh letter from Cynthia Ozick in which she reproached me because I claim we should separate a writer's artistic activity from his political opinions: "Why? Are we talking about two different people? What do you mean by this?"

HS: Here in America you were reproached for being much too tolerant. You tiptoed around a pot of boiling porridge, as it were.

NM: *The Los Angeles Times* even wrote that I eulogized Mircea Eliade. Here I was considered much too cautions, too nuanced, too careful. Over there I was considered a traitor—a Jewish traitor.

HS: Because you shoved the great hero of Romanian culture off his pedestal. In our conversation you recalled that at the beginning you didn't want to accept the invitation to write about Eliade. You knew what you would expose. Was this the reason you were excessively cautious?

NM: Yes. And I as told you, notwithstanding, the caution wasn't of any use to me. I was coming from a society in which everything was politicized. Even when politics wasn't being talked about, things were interpreted in a political way. I could no longer stand the exclusivity of certain simplistic, excessive, reductive, and unacceptable political positions. I didn't want to be like them. I didn't want to be like those cultural political activists that pick over everything we write three times, as if hunting for fleas, until they find something to cling to.

HS: Anyhow, in the case of Mircea Eliade, we have to be allowed to ask ourselves if there isn't, nevertheless, a connection between his admiration for the Iron Guard and his body of work.

N.M: Here we have to talk about another critic of mine, the French scholar Daniel Dubuisson. He wrote a book, *Mythologies of the Twentieth Century*, in which there is a chapter dedicated to Eliade. Dubuisson tries to create a connection between Eliade's vision of the history of religions and his fascist political convictions. Dubuisson criticizes me both because I distinguished between Eliade's way of seeing history and his convictions, and because I did not touch on Eliade's work—not even his artistic work, in which signs of his conception of fascism could be found as well. Is Dubuisson right or not? I don't know.

I wrote my article at a time when there did not yet exist a bibliography of, or complete research into, Eliade's work. I based myself, in the first place, on what I knew, and I used the biography of an admirer of his, a former student. There I found several quotations that I was able to use, but it was difficult. Two decades have gone by since my article appeared. Meanwhile, it has been proved not only that I was absolutely right—although I had been called a liar in Romania—but also that many more things were unknown or hidden. New information was discovered. I had had a correct intuition, but it provoked a huge scandal.

HS: The Romanian Parliament was offering homage back then to Antonescu. Isn't that so?

NM: By 1990, I think, Antonescu's name had even been given to some streets, as well. Why? Because Antonescu was anti-communist. And what was Eliade? An anti-communist. This fact was more important than anything else.

HS: Doesn't there exist a tradition of democratic, liberal anti-communism in Romania? Or of a leftist anti-communism? George Orwell was a radical Socialist until the day he died, and he wrote *Nineteen Eighty-Four*, perhaps the best anti-communist novel.

NM: That is exactly what I asked after 1989. Why do you resuscitate the extreme right? Why don't you look for real democrats in the Romanian tradition? In Ceauşescu's time there existed a leftist, anti-communist group. For Romania it was very unusual, almost bizarre, because there hadn't existed a very powerful leftist tradition. *Aktionsgruppe Banat* was made up of young leftist intellectuals, ethnic Germans, who criticized the Romanian dictatorship from a Marxist perspective. For the Romanian government they were even more dangerous than the opposition on the right. They were condemned, arrested. Many of them emigrated to Germany.

Romania was always a country in which nationalism was powerful, and thus anti-communist. Just think of the following statistics: After the Second World War, the Romanian Communist Party had barely a thousand members. They were a small organization, an insignificant sect. In 1989, the Romanian Communist Party was the largest communist party in Eastern Europe, with almost four million members. But among the members you wouldn't find so much as one thousand real communists! Almost all of them became members of the party for opportunistic motives: They needed a party card to find better jobs so that their children might go to university. This had nothing to do with their own beliefs. One day after Ceauşescu's death, many were already anti-communists, and all of them were claiming to have been victims, even the Securitate informers and members of the Central Committee. And I don't say they weren't victims, in a way! Only that they were another kind of victims than those who landed in prison or were persecuted. And a part of those who considered themselves victims became Nationalists, including greater and lesser members of the *Nomenklatura*.

HS: In this atmosphere, your article landed like a bomb.

NM: If the same text were published today, reactions would of course be more moderate, although echoes of the explosion back then persist even today. The fact that few today doubt anymore that Eliade was close to the Iron Guard doesn't count; I remain the same monster.

Let's take a charming example, an attack that comes not from some stupid nationalists and anti-Semites but from a well-known literary critic who maintains, serenely, that it is natural that the United States of America, which has not yet assumed its own guilt for the Vietnam War and the massacre of the Indians, should turn its attention toward the Holocaust and should invent guilty parties in order to turn the direction of public debate. No more, no less! As you know, Dadaism had its own destiny in Romania.

HS: In other words, you wrote the article for *The New Republic* on orders from the CIA, which wanted to deflect attention from the My Lai massacre. How much did the CIA pay you?

NM: Very well. It's an institution with a lot of money. Look where I live: I'm the embodiment of the American dream. You can't realize the American dream without the help of the CIA. Even our mutual friend Eliade may have needed the help from the CIA. After he was invited to the University of Chicago, he wrote in his journal, "They'll never admit me. I won't get a visa." Perhaps you recall that in the visa request it says, "If you were ever a member of or sympathizer with a totalitarian organization, the visa is refused." Eliade had supported the Iron Guard at a time when Romania was still a parliamentary democracy, weak and corrupt be it said, but from a juridical point of view it was not yet a dictatorship. The American authorities believe that someone who became a Nazi before Hitler came to power is guiltier that a person who became a Nazi after Germany became a single party state. The same criterion is valid for Romania as well, and it's *not* a stupid criterion.

Eliade belonged to a category of persons who were not at all welcome here in America. How was he nevertheless able to integrate, from a social point of view?

HS: He lied somehow on the visa request?

NM: I don't know. I said only in farcical jest that even he needed the help of the CIA. I was the same, as you suspect. They paid me and inspired me, they created a special professorial position for me, and I gave monthly information about everything that happened at Bard College with these crazy leftist students, be they Bangladeshi or Arab or Israeli. That's my connection with the CIA. And in Romania, you have to acknowledge, I did a very good job for them!

–The Fourteenth Dialogue–
On Celan, Fondane, and Cioran

HS: What kind of relationship did you have with Paul Celan?

NM: He always preoccupied me, and I have had a lot to do with him recently. I wrote an essay about him that I published in a volume called *Laptele Negru* (*The Black Milk*)—an allusion to Celan's poem *Todesfuge* (*Deathfuge*)—in which I found myself imagining a postmortem meeting between Celan and the poet Benjamin Fondane. The essay exists as a paraphrase of Celan's single prose text: *Conversation in the Mountains*[6]. Celan and Fondane both spent their last days in Paris. Both came from Romania—one from Bucovina; the other from Moldova, the adjacent region. One died in the Seine, drowned; the other, Fondane, was burned at Auschwitz. Thus one died in water, the other in fire.

Their poems are very different. Fondane was a Romanian-French poet, a close friend of the Christianized Jewish Russian existentialist Lev Isaakovici Shestov. Initially, Fondane signed his name "Fundoianu," until he left Romania in the '20s, explaining that he no longer wanted to live in a French colony. He preferred the metropolis itself. Until he met Shestov—and became his friend and most important partner in discussion—Fondane published a great deal in the Jewish press in Romania. One of his essays had the same theme as a book of Shestov's, *Athens and Jerusalem*, in which the ancient Greeks and Hebrews were seen as the core of European culture.

I wrote about Celan and Fondane as outstanding examples of Jewish-Romanian writers in exile who created in another language[7]; Fondane in French, Celan in German. Fondane was a victim of the Holocaust; Celan likewise, in another fashion. As a poet Celan was so obsessively preoccupied with this tragedy that he lived it to excess through his traumatic poetry.

HS: Didn't he suffer all his life from the oppressive feeling that he left his parents to a hard fate, because he survived while they were killed?

---

6   "Beyond the Mountains" may be read in English in *The Fifth Impossibility* (Yale University Press, 2012)

7   In 2008, at the Babes-Bolyai University in Cluj, in my speech of thanks for the honorary degree I received there, I spoke about Paul Celan, and at the Alex I. Cuza University in Iași, in 2012, at a similar event, I spoke about Benjamin Fondane (Note 2012, NM).

NM: Yes, he suffered, but his suffering went beyond personal tragedy. Celan buried himself in this tragic Jewish destiny, and he transformed it into his principal topic—often highly codified—and into a lyrical expression that is not transitive: a personal, secret language that sometimes becomes esoteric, even if Celan could not bear this characterization.

HS: Some of Celan's work doesn't seem at all esoteric to me. When, for example, he says in his poem "*Late and Deep,* "At the mills of death ye grind the white meal of the Promise," the point is as clear as can be. You would have to enroll voluntarily in the SS, like the German literary critic Hans Egon Holthusen, not to notice that "the mills of death" represent the German extermination camps.

NM: Of course. And the formulation "Death is a Master from Germany," from *Todesfuge,* is clear enough. You don't have to be a highly refined literary spirit to get it. Apropos, do you know that *Todesfuge* was first published in Bucharest, in Romanian, in the translation of Petre Solomon, a friend of Celan's who was himself a poet? The title was *Tangoul morţi (Death Tango).* The poem appeared in an important literary review, *Contemporanul (The Contemporary),* in a period when this kind of poetry could not be published, not even under the pretext of anti-fascism. Of course *Todesfuge* is an anti-fascist poem. But it is also very much more than that.

After the war, Paul Celan lived in Bucharest for several years, and was close to a group of young Surrealist poets, many of them Jewish. He worked for a publishing house that published Russian literature in translation. Celan would later call the period spent in Romania "the period of the *calembour* (the pun)." In any event, Celan felt that right after the war he had had a wonderful time in Bucharest—at a time he was writing poems in Romanian. For this reason, I included him as a Romanian poet in an anthology that I recently published in America[8]—as a Romanian poet.

H.S: Paul Celan translated E.M. Cioran's *Treatise on Decomposition* from the Romanian.

---

8   *Romanian Writers on Writing (The Writer's World),* Trinity University Press 2011. Celan's essay is titled "Partisan of the Erotical Absolute."

NM: And he was terribly affected when he found that Cioran was close to the Iron Guard.

HS: I have read Patrice Bollon's biography of Cioran. It seems that Cioran was even crazier, even more to the extreme right than Eliade. How can that be? Is it even possible?

NM: It was possible. It would be understatement to describe some of his statements as scandalous. Cioran's second language was German, not French, as is commonly thought. Cioran had a scholarship in Germany when Hitler was at the height of his power. He sent back letters from Berlin claiming that Hitler was the greatest man in history because he had managed to annihilate the critical spirit in Germany. And he wrote the following sentence: "If I were to choose between Jesus and the Captain," by which he means Codreanu, the leader of the Iron Guard, "I would choose the Captain."

And he wrote other, similarly delirious phrases. Unlike Eliade, Cioran was a nihilist. In a book known in English as *Transfiguration of Romania* (and whose title might be better translated as *Romania's Changing Face* or *Changing the Face of Romania*), Cioran maintains that if we want to change this country, we have to burn it down first.

HS: Cioran was a self-loathing Romanian.

NM: He was an ultranationalist by way of sky-high ultra-nihilism. He wasn't Eliade, who says, "We will build a wonderful country, ours alone, a star." Cioran wouldn't ever have written anything like that. His opinion was always that we're all a bunch of crap, the biggest pile of crap in the world. And he said of the Jews, "We can't keep up with them."

HS: This was also the opinion of Wilhelm Marr, who introduced the word 'anti-Semitism' into German. In his manifesto *The Victory of Judaism over Germanism—Seen from a Non-confessional Point of View*, he wrote words to this effect: "We poor, stupid Germans, we don't measure up to the Jews. Anti-Semitism is our last, desperate line of defense."

NM: This was Cioran's attitude, too. There's a distinction between this attitude and Eliade's phrase, "We don't want to be invaded, either by Jews or syphilis." I don't say that Cioran's attitude wasn't anti-Semitic, but he didn't consider Jews insects or a disease; he believed that, being a very ancient people, the Jews know everything. He wrote ugly things, rather, about the Romanians, about the Slavs—about everyone, more or less—even about the French.

He was not an infantile Nationalist of the kind that bids up his co-nationals, but he believed that only the Iron Guard could clean out the national garbage. When he was young, he used to incite the slaughter of old people. "Out with them! We are young. We don't need them! Enough, already! Kill them! Execute them en masse." With him it wasn't just the Jews who were a problem; it was the whole world.

HS: This youth cult is to be found among the Nazis too. Most of them were young when Hitler came to power. The Nazis were against static, moldy, reactionary matters: against the aristocrats, against the monarchists. In fact, Christianity seemed reactionary to them.

NM: Here is the essential distinction between the Nazis and the Iron Guard: Among all the fascist movements, the Iron Guard was the only one with a religious ideology. I'm reminded more of Al-Qaida than of Hitler.

HS: And E. M. Cioran hated himself not only as a Romanian but also as a Christian. While he was the son of an Orthodox priest, in his entire body of work he speaks about Christianity exclusively with disgust.

NM: Absolutely. Mircea Eliade was an Iron Guard sympathizer, whereas Emil Cioran was, I'd say, a nihilistic rebel. Cioran, Eliade, and other Legionnaires were obsessed with the idea of death. Death for them is the happy dream and the perfection, the culmination of life. The elegizing of death, sacrifice, martyrdom—thus of the collective dead—can be found in the Nazis and again in fanatic Islamists. Cioran held these ideas, it is true, but later he was very disturbed by the stupidity of the ideas of his youth, not necessarily by how sinister they were. In his journal, he describes telephone conversations with Eugen Ionescu, whom he keeps asking, "How could I really have been that stupid?" Ionescu always answered the same way: "You were crazy."

HS: Cioran didn't hide his fascist past?

NM: He recalled it somewhat in his little book *My Country*, where he tried to explain his fascination with the Iron Guard.

HS: You visited Cioran, no? How was it?

NM: My connection with him was arranged by a friend of his from Paris, Edouard Roditi, who was teaching at Bard College where he was a guest professor, very much a man of the world. He wrote to Cioran that we had met, and Cioran answered in a very flattering way: "As it happens I've just received the latest issue of *Accents* [*Akzente*] magazine, and I read Norman Manea's text 'Romania: Three Lines with Commentary,' the best thing that I've ever read about our country." His friend asked me to send Cioran a few lines, and Cioran replied in a very friendly way. In a letter to me he wrote, "You should move to Paris; it's the best place to waste your life." Very typical of him.

When I was in Paris, I rang him; he invited us for dinner. He was friendly, delicate and pleasant. He was not at all the individual whose name stands over those tough, instigative texts. No! I knew that he refused to speak Romanian, but on that evening he spoke Romanian.

HS: Did you like him?

NM: Yes, yes, he was charming.

HS: Did you discuss the "Jewish Question"?

NM: I didn't want to open that discussion—nor did he say a word about it. At a certain moment he began to speak about his friend Constantin Noica, an important philosopher, himself a former sympathizer with the Iron Guard. Cioran's famous "Letter to a Distant Friend," published in the *Nouvelle Revue Français*, was addressed to Noica, who had remained in Romania. Naïvely sent by post, Noica's letter in reply became "open" itself when the censors read it, and an appalling trial followed. Noica was condemned to many years of imprisonment, and was freed after eight or nine. After that, he became duplicitous: He made a secret pact with the system, as did many former detainees in communist prisons.

At one point during our evening, Cioran asked, "You know what Noica does when he comes to visit me in Paris? He notes down everything I say, for his report to Securitate." I smiled. The situation was, at least, peculiar. Cioran was seeing me for the first time and hadn't the least reason to trust me. He was talking about his Legionnaire friend with a stranger—who, on top of that, was also a Jew.

HS: Doesn't he somehow write that Romanians can only trust Jews?

NM: Yes, and that's an odd sentence too. In another place he writes, "If you want to tell someone a secret and be sure that person won't spread it further, there's only one solution: Kill him." That was Cioran! On his deathbed he was visited by a Jewish-Romanian writer who lived in Israel. When he was young and a communist, this writer had written a very tough text against Cioran. Now he wanted to have another word with the sick man. Moribund, Cioran managed to say only several words: "You should know that I was never an anti-Semite." In his journal he wrote that he was a metaphysical Jew. You could even believe this if you didn't read further. A few pages beyond, he says that he's a Mongol.

–The Fifteenth Dialogue–
A Letter to No One

HS: How do you write? By hand, on the typewriter, or on a laptop?

NM: In Romania I used to write by hand, and a typist copied texts for me. That was the custom in Romania. Then I managed to buy myself a small typewriter made in the German Democratic Republic, and I typed a few texts, but never books of fiction or essays. As you may know, in Romania it was forbidden to keep a typewriter if you didn't present yourself with it at the police station to pass a kind of test every year, after which the police retained a copy with all the typewriter's characters. All the letters of the alphabet were struck, plus a text or two. Then you'd receive a written authorization allowing you to retain this explosive machine. It was an interesting and deplorable spectacle. You'd see people of advanced age carrying their heavy, old typewriters. This says something about the system, I hope.

HS: The point of this exercise was for the government to know the kind of letters and signs on every typewriter in the entire country.

NM: Exactly. When I arrived in America, I bought myself an electric typewriter or two, at first a heavy old one, solid and trustworthy; then a more modern one. Here I no longer had a lady to type my texts. I became my own secretary, and my own copyeditor and proofreader. Later I bought an electric typewriter with which you could erase two lines—so it had a small memory. In the end, my friend Philip Roth pushed me to buy a computer. I bought myself one along with him—but he, as a much more organized and disciplined American, hired someone to teach him how to use the damned thing. I was self-taught. I learned how the computer works as I did a typewriter: step by step.

Then computers began to evolve. I stayed with my old model for a long time, though in the meantime I've also changed several times, but I'm not very good at this device.

HS: Are you one of the people who revise your material a lot as you write?

NM: Yes. I have revised older books too, for an edition of my collected work that my Romanian publisher is bringing out.

HS: How important is construction for you?

NM: Very important. For example, I found the structure for *The Hooligan's Return* late in the process, when I was finishing writing, almost at the end, and I was only satisfied when I saw the unity of the four parts. Only then did I reckon I had really finished.

HS: If the structure came so late, how did you begin, then?

NM: I hesitated a great deal over the writing of this book. I struggled with my editor Roger Strauss, a good friend and a good publisher, who had ask me to write precisely this book of memories. I wanted to write not an autobiography but a novel. It seems to me that I spend too much time on essays here in exile. I wanted to return to narration. But in the end I gave in.

It's very hard for me to start a book. Time goes by, until my intentions become clear and the writing starts to flow. I began *The Hooligan's Return*; then I changed everything around until I found the right beginning. The book's first chapter, "Barney Greengrass," which describes a New York morning during which the narrator, a refugee, meets with an American friend, was not the original beginning. Later, it seemed to fit there as an anecdotal element, so to speak.

HS: What are you writing, right now?

NM: *The Lair*, a novel. I still have to do some finishing work, some modifications, but it's essentially done. It's a novel about exile and the refuge that literature and reading may constitute in exile. You find friends in an unknown environment, which is to say you find old books that you already know, books that you read in the past and that you rediscover now. It's a kind of intellectual thriller.[9]

9 *Vizuina* (*The Lair*), Yale 2012

HS: What's the scenario of this thriller?

NM: It has a connection to something that happened to me at Bard College, when I received a written death threat.

HS: Recently?

NM: No, years ago.

HS: In connection with the article about Eliade?

NM: So I believed, and it became a source of stress for me because Eliade's friend and disciple Professor Ioan P. Culianu was shot in Chicago in 1991. The death threat letter was peculiar. It contained a quotation from Jorge Luis Borges, from his story "Death and the Compass." In the end it turned out that the whole thing was just a farce. The threatening letter was one of the forty letters sent by a student at Bard, a young Muslim lady who wanted to organize an exhibition, an "installation."

This scenario confers a certain dynamism on the novel, but there's more than that. It's about exile, love, illness, solitude, death.

HS: We've talked about the fact that construction is important for you. How do you discover a scenario?

NM: By chance or through imagination.

HS: I know that there are two kinds of writers: Some need to know the whole story by heart, mentally, before sitting down to put a word on paper. Others let themselves be carried along. To use a metaphor, they enter an appallingly dark forest and come out at the other end with a book in hand—or nothing. Which category do you belong to?

NM: Neither, or both. I don't have everything clearly in mind when I start to write. I have the pretext, the motivation. A lot of things show up along the way from the epic material itself. The moment you find that the book is already leading you, it means you're on the right road. I need an enigma, a stimulus, something that pushes me to write. I don't blindly enter this unknown terrain in the hope that I'll find something. Although I believe, too, that a text may be obtained by the second method, everything depends on the particular case, which means the type of author but also the type of narrative.

HS: Your book *October, Eight O'Clock* can't be easily categorized. It could be called a collection of stories, or a novel made of conjoined fragments.

NM: Claudio Magris liked it a lot. It's a book of separate stories, linked by the same main character and gathered together in a kind of Bildungsroman. The texts were published at different moments. There's no continuity of writing, but taken together the composition may be considered a novel in which the narrative fragments exist as unconventional chapters. I made the selection of texts in the latest German edition from Hanser Verlag with the editor, but I regret that my novella *The Trenchcoat* isn't in this book, or republished independently. I think it's a good text.

HS: What's that book about?

NM: About the terror in a closed society. A trench coat shows up by chance after a dinner party at the residence of an official writer. Three couples dined together at the party. The trenchcoat is found the next day. No one claims it. No one asks, and no one comes for it. The hostess, the writer's wife, becomes gradually obsessed by the event, which leaves her anxious, traumatized, suspicious. The story begins with an enigma—which is never, for that matter, unraveled—and it shows us the way in which the characters react in this situation, in a police state that swarms with spies and informers who may be among one's close friends and associates. Gradually, gradually, the characters and the relations among them unfold, but the special revelation is the insidious terror of daily life in a closed, totalitarian society.

HS: If today you were to rewrite the books that you wrote and published in Romania, would they be much different?

NM: They would be more open, probably, since I no longer live under censorship and because the Anglo-Saxon way of writing has begun to influence me—though only somewhat—a result of the more concrete focus and a style that's more direct than the hyper-complicated Central and Eastern European way of writing. I can't assess the extent to which the books written here show any change, or how marked the change is.

We may ask what will survive of the codified way of writing accomplished under censorship. Increasingly, current consumer literature is developing in the direction of journalism or autobiography. Surely part of yesterday's literature will disappear; another part will remain only as the document of a certain epoch, of a certain way of living, writing, and reading. Censorship used to provoke tricks of codification through which the writer defended himself—including through metaphor—strategic dodges that could sometimes be more powerful than direct story telling by dint of the mystery, the obscurity, the provocation, the charade they involved.

HS: Has your encounter with Anglo-Saxon literature made you become less equivocal?

NM: I remain—for better or worse—equivocal, and I am probably a complicated Central European writer. But I have felt challenged by what people here in America understand by the essay, by the story. And the translations of my texts have played a certain role. I was intimidated because, in the case of a complicated text, the danger of losing a great deal as a result of bad translation is much greater than in the case of a simple text. When I tried to write ever more simply, I wound up disappointed with myself; I was simplifying and simplifying until there no longer remained very much of me. That danger may exist even now, but I don't believe that my way of writing has been essentially transformed.

HS: What leaps to my attention when I compare your earlier texts with the later ones is the fact that is that the later ones are more jocular, even if in a very somber and sardonic way.

NM: Humor, satire, whatever you want to call them, are the result of some distancing. When hope is gone, all that remains is sardonic laughter.

HS: The Viennese say, "The situation is hopeless, but it's not serious."

NM: The situation can be serious, too, but when there is no longer any solution, then one must become ironic—even with regard to oneself. This has to do with the way in which people treat the power that oppresses them, as well. If you see the oppressor's importance in an exclusively tragic mode, then, to a certain extent, you legitimize it. If you try to see the oppressor in a satiric light, to transform that authority at least partially into something grotesque or ridiculous, then you diminish its importance a bit.

Yes, it's true that this dimension of my work became more important in America.

HS: Are you happy when you write?

NM: There exist moments of joy, of triumph. Moments of liberation—you're happy when your sentence has worked out, when you've written a good page. It's hard work. It requires enormous concentration. This isn't happiness in the usual sense of the word. You don't feel like dancing when you've written a good page. If, however, you put in the final period and it seems to you that you have an okay book, one that works, that gives you a sense of contentment.

HS: George Orwell said in his essay "Why I Write" that motives that are not precisely noble push the writer to his table: "*sheer egotism,*" the need to feel yourself important and to shine before others; "*aesthetic enthusiasm*"; and desire for revenge. Do you agree?

NM: In any case, I agree with the fact that it is not unfailingly a matter of a noble mission, an obligation toward humanity, at whose disposition you place the great fruits of your thought and creativity so as to correct the sins of the world. Socialist propaganda used to consider the writer "an engineer of the human soul," to use the words of the great Joseph Vissarionovich: the writer as educator and reformer, with a responsibility to the masses. I believe the writer is mainly responsible to himself. Perhaps some of the reasons that make a writer write are among those Orwell names. Out of desire for revenge—it may happen in some cases, but I don't think that desire predominates. In the end what counts is the literary product, and when you take vengeance you don't do yourself any service. The text may become stupid, and turn against the author himself.

I still believe that one of the principle reasons for writing is a profound discontent with what daily chaos has to offer us. We need something else that transcends this chaos, either to give it a meaning or to add another reality to reality. Religion, too, responds to this need, as do other therapies of solitude. All this is a matter of a letter addressed to no one, to a virtual partner. You feel the need to add something to the daily waste of time, of life—because the whole thing goes by too fast. The search for lost time is the search for meaning.

–THE SIXTEENTH DIALOGUE–
On Nabokov

HS: OK, let's talk about Vladimir Nabokov's novel *Pnin*. What interests you about it? The fact that, like yourself, Timofey Pavlovich Pnin is a refugee who succeeded in America?

NM: I like this book very much. I like the main character. I'm interested not only in the clownish figure of the Russian intellectual lost in exile, but also in a very intelligent strategy employed by the author, who introduces a narrator who resembles himself—a Russian emigrant writer who has achieved success and whom he also undermines, so that in the end you can't completely believe what he says. A great question mark floats over the narrative. It's a very original and intelligent trick: The reader is caught in an equivocal state while, through his awkwardness and aloneness, the main character, a charming failure, imposes himself before the socially successful author, who gradually loses the reader's sympathy because he isn't trustworthy, because he is deceptive, too intelligent in using his social opportunities, an imposing *macher*. Pnin is his opposite, an odd duck, shy and sensitive, and still the reader addresses his sympathy to him in the end. The storyteller has manipulated it in Pnin's direction, and estranged it from himself. To me, it seems an original and stimulating situation.

HS: What does Nabokov mean to you?

NM: Usually he is offered as an example of a writer who succeeded in passing, brilliantly and seemingly inexplicably, from one language to another. Things don't stand quite that way. That is cliché spread by those who have no idea what is at issue. At the age of 16 Nabokov was a student at Cambridge. He is not a Russian emigrant who came to the West and passed suddenly from one language to another. He grew up in a cultivated, wealthy, almost aristocratic Russian family. From the time he was small he had French, English and German teachers—before learning Russian. Of course, he has a great talent for languages. That's clear. His style is brilliant, not only in *Pnin* but also in *Lolita* and the other novels.

For me he is an example of a democratic Russian. Westernized, alien to the traditional nationalism of Russian intellectuals. His father was killed by them—

HS: His father fled from Bolsheviks. He was a "white," and a convinced liberal.

NM: He was part of the cultivated intellectual class, but he was not among the reactionary, anti-Semitic whites.

I feel close to a poem that Nabokov wrote in Russian, when he was living, I believe, in Berlin. The poem is addressed to the Russian language. "Free me!" the verse asks, addressing itself to the Russian language. "Let me free. Let me leave." The lamentation is born of concatenation: the Russian language is in him; it remains in him; it is him. He experiences it as a burden, a dear pressure to which he is enthralled, fascinated, and which, at the same time, he can not bear.

HS: This describes your relationship with Romanian.

NM: Yes, but I don't have Nabokov's possibilities for escape; I cannot write poetry or fiction in English. I can only write epistles or essays, and I can speak English or German with Mr. Hannes Stein, the journalist, in America. Still, there exists something that can't be healed: the pith of your soul, the language that grew along with you from childhood.

HS: Nabokov's real invention isn't the storyteller who inspires distrust but the criminal storyteller. I'm thinking of Humbert Humbert in *Lolita*, but also of Hermann, the storyteller from *Despair*. It seems to me that this masquerade is a trick: Nabokov poses as an aesthete who is not interested in morality at all. You don't have to dig far, though, to discover a moral vision of the world behind this pose.

NM: It's an interesting theme. From a moral point of view you may protect yourself from evil, even through aestheticism, through an aesthetic— defending yourself from the pollution of politics, from the aggression of the social abyss—in this way situating yourself morally on the good side without being a rhetorician of morality. In Romania I wrote an essay about what I called *est-etica* [a play on words combining the meanings "Eastern-aesthetic" and "Eastern-ethic"], which is to say an aesthetic that includes a morality, an ethic. If you were an aesthete in a totalitarian communist system that stigmatized aestheticism, as did the socialist East, that involved risks as well. It meant that you kept your distance, solitude, independence, morality. The aesthete wasn't serving the party and moral sloganeers. He maintained his independence of spirit, his creativity. This was, in the given situation, an act of heroism.

Of course, some people criticize Nabokov for his elitist attitude, but the story of his life and work belongs to an admirable writer. I like his passion for butterflies, too.

HS: How so?

NM: I once wanted to write more about him, and I read his research on butterflies. At a certain moment I was in Lausanne, at the museum that houses his butterfly collection. I confess that I was disappointed; I didn't find one spectacular butterfly there. There were only small butterflies, and they weren't very colorful. Nabokov was a recognized researcher in the field, almost a scientist. Butterflies were his passion, his hobby, but it went far beyond a simple hobby. I'm pleased by this extraordinary symbol for beauty and art, for something as charming and ephemeral as a butterfly. This side of him always moved me.

If we want to stay on our Jewish theme, I could add that Nabokov was always an anti-anti-Semite.

HS: He was married to a Jewish woman.

NM: This may be a reason for someone's becoming an anti-Semite, too, however. I don't know if the Romanian writer Paul Goma wrote some anti-Semitic texts after 1989 for this reason. No, I would prefer to think there are other causes. In Nabokov's case, his Jewish wife was everything to him: lover, friend, wife, literary adviser.

–THE SEVENTEENTH DIALOGUE–
A Proust from the East

HS: Is Romania happy about the Nobel Prize for Literature Herta Müller received?

NM: Not very. However, it seems better than if the prize had been granted to Norman Manea. For more than ten years, a part of the Romanian press has been wringing its hands, desperate lest such a misfortune befall. I would steal the great crown that Romania has been wanting for almost a hundred years—I, the Jew, the American, the traitor to the nation, the foreigner, the enemy. Happily, the thing hasn't happened, and Romania blooms anew.

HS: I think they went a bit haywire when Imre Kertész won the Nobel Prize.

NM: And when Elfriede Jelinek won the Nobel Prize—and Harold Pinter—there was great agitation. "A Jew again! Who else is missing?"[10] I was missing. Romanian newspapers keep repeating that I'm famous, the most translated Romanian author. I have replied to these fears with the solemn promise that I'd do everything possible to get Romania out of this scrape. There are indications that I'll succeed. And if the great misfortune should happen, though, in the end, I will take the Fatherland's sensibilities into consideration and not present myself as a Romanian writer.

HS: Let's talk about another Jew who didn't win the Nobel Prize: Marcel Proust. It seems to me that you are a bit reserved about Proust. In *The Hooligan's Return* it says, for example, that your problem was never the fact that your mother didn't give you a goodnight kiss. In another place you describe your "madeleine": a bit of sugar that hung from the roof attached to a piece of twine.

---

10   The "Jewish Nobel" doesn't seem to be only a Romanian obsession. It's probably worth reading the essay "Un nouveau révisionnisme: le prix Nobel et le juifs" (*Le Monde*, 07.04.2011).

NM: In my book *October, Eight O'Clock* there's a story called "Proust's Tea." It describes the moment in which the camp survivors are brought into a waiting room in a train station. A lady from the Red Cross has brought them tea. The little boy from the camp drinks the tea; let's call it the tea of happiness. The titles' role is to suggest a comparison with the tea in which the little boy Marcel dips his madeleine. The tea of the little boy escaped from the camp is drunk in a completely other geographical and historical situation. He's a Jewish boy—as was Proust, who had a Jewish mother, too—but the survivor's mother is aged and diminished—a dwarf, almost—and the little boy is a dwarf too. Both returned from hell as skeletons. It's a matter of the contrast between two very different premises in which a child's sensibility is formed.

I was and am a great admirer of Proust. I encountered him in the '60s—no, in the mid-to-late '50s—when I was a student in Bucharest and I had access to big libraries. I read him in a wonderful Romanian translation; I was completely absorbed by *In Search of Lost Time*. Biography and history, however, pushed me rather closer to Kafka, although structurally I was closer to Proust. Life—the dictatorship, the camps, the situation of Jews in Eastern Europe—made me closer to Kafka.

Because you are more interested in the writer than his disease—his writing, that is—I'll tell you a story. Several years ago some Romanian friends convinced me to look for my Securitate file. In the end I gave in, and pages selected by the current officers of a special service were sent to me. They lacked essential episodes of my relations with our adorable protector of yesterday and today, Securitate. I found something sensational, however: the medical document drawn up when I came back to Romania from the camp. I was nine years old. When I arrived in Romania the Red Cross took me in charge. I had a medical consultation with doctors, who recorded the results.

HS: Which were now found in your Securitate file.

NM: The medical document of a little boy, of a child of nine years. He wasn't a dissident yet. He wasn't a Zionist, communist, or a believer. He was just a wretched Jewish boy returned from a concentration camp. There were several ordinary observations in the document—he's thin, needs food, vitamins—and the document was kept with great care in my Securitate file for so many years. For any eventuality! I didn't know anything about this document, nor did my parents know a thing. Only the police already knew something essential about me. But that boy was not Marcel Proust.

HS: Maybe another Proust.

NM: Who knows? You're speaking only of a potential Marcel Proust, not from Paris, but from the East.

A Conversation Between
Norman Manea and Ilana Shmueli

Jerusalem, December 2009

Norman Manea: How changed was he? I don't mean only with respect to his age.

Ilana Shmueli: My first meeting with Paul after the war was in Paris.

NM: When was this?

IS: Before the Six-Day War, I believe, in Fall '65, I traveled to Paris. I had already been to Europe several times, but this was my first visit to Paris. Celan's address and telephone number were given to me by a mutual friend. Celan's number was a secret. The first evening I walked around Paris alone. It was late summer. I looked him up, but no one was at home, and I left a message with my phone number and the address of my hotel on his door. Then we met, for the first time in twenty-one years. Indeed I found him very changed—somewhat carelessly dressed and much heavier than I remembered him. He approached me openly and with joy. He was, at the time, about fifty, and I was forty-five.

NM: No longer very young.

IS: No longer very young. Yet it was a good reunion, which then became a bit complicated, since both of us, after all, were complicated. (We already knew this from our time in Czernowitz.) The initial sense of estrangement rapidly resolved, and almost from the first moment we found our common language. Everything went smoothly, and we had a lot to tell each other. We met in the late afternoon and walked all night through the streets of Paris. He suggested that I make secret wishes on coins and toss them into the Seine from the Pont Neuf. Early in the morning, we arrived at Les Halles. Celan bought me a bundle of radishes instead of flowers and we were happy. Then naturally we ate onion soup—which of course belonged to his time in Paris.

NM: And your meeting in Jerusalem?

IS: That was about three years later. In Paris, when we parted I had promised him that if he were to come to Israel I would be his "guide" in Jerusalem, as wonderful a guide as he had been for me on this night in Paris. After this meeting, we wrote several letters to each other. And after his death his

103

wife found an unsent letter from this time, which she gave to me, along with all my own letters. In that letter he informs me of a possible visit to Jerusalem.

NM: As I told you before, I was very impressed by these letters, I even had the feeling they should be similar to Milena's (lost) letters to Kafka. This very deep connection—how to describe it?—a dialogue that was no dialogue and yet was more than a dialogue. What they say, what don't say, and how that dialogue is understood by both correspondents is deeply moving.

IS: For me he was not really so difficult to understand. I think we were very close; there were many similarities between us. Although externally I mostly behaved as one who fit in. I did not feel free to live and act out my own peculiarly individual personality traits, as I would have liked to do, and as he mostly did.

NM: Yes, I understand.

IS: Very often he seized the right to behave according to his moods, and these were not always very congenial and not always pleasant. Already in Czernowitz, in the ghetto, we discovered that in our emotional world we had a lot in common—volatility, ambiguity, hypersensitivity, contradictoriness. He found me "cheeky" (which I was, too) and overly critical. Later, when I read his letters and poems, I often had the feeling that I, myself, would have to write this. I felt it as a part of me—now, I know, this is presumptuous. I discovered something strange in these last days. I am now working on a short afterword for the little volume, *Say that Jerusalem Is*. My publisher wants to release a new edition. Going through the little book I found the poem:

> *Einen Stiefel voll Hirn*
> *in den Regen gestellt.*
> *Es wird ein Gehn sein, ein großes*
> *weit über die Grenzen,*
> *die uns ziehn.*

It struck me that I had recorded "Gehn sein" as *one single* word in the epilogue. As a stopping, a halting, a self-continuing state of being, thus *ein großes Gehnsein*, "a great goingbeing." It was a neologism, which to me seemed very natural for Celan. Especially these poems—whose contexts I knew and whose creation I had been present for—seemed very close to me.

NM: Were you prepared at that moment to give shelter to such a soul as he was? Was this an expectation; was this also perhaps a wish, a desire to receive—shall we say—such a complicated yet brotherly soul?

IS: Ever since our time in Czernowitz he has remained alive in me. There we were part of a group that came together to read and discuss things with one another, but Paul was for me—and not only for me—the center. Then what came simply came.

NM: I suspect in Paris he was not the same person as in Czernowitz. Was there a great change? And was there an expectation?

IS: Apparently there were some sorts of expectations, representations had been made. A mutual friend (still from the time in the ghetto) came at that time from Paris and told me a lot about him. He brought me a handwritten copy of "*Todesfuge*" and also a copy of "The Meridian." I understood little at the time. Yet as I read "The Meridian" over again following our meetings and conversations, it grew different. I also desired and anticipated these conversations. His texts spoke to me very directly, even if I often did not wholly comprehend them.

NM: Of course in his case there was a code, and step by step one had to learn to break the code in order to understand it.

IS: Yes, there were also codes that were entirely our own. When he began to send me the poems, those he said he had written for me, I had the feeling of intimacy—of knowledge. I, too, had experienced, had been present when they arose, in their creation. When I was in Paris, he read aloud for me his last two books, already prepared for publication, *Lichtzwang* [*Lightduress*] and *Schneepart* [*Snowpart*]. He read me each of these books twice in succession, one after the other, the whole book, without interruption. And I asked nothing, not a thing. Nor did I have any need to ask questions, although I knew that this would be a fantastic opportunity to talk about his poetry. He would rarely speak about his poems, and I knew this. He wanted to read and read.

NM: He did not want to explain himself.

IS: He did not want to explain himself, but for example, the first poem that we were still reading together in Jerusalem, *"Du sei wie du, immer"* ["You be like you, always"] is not a simple poem. We spoke a great deal about it, but it was a talk *with* the poem and not *about* the poem.

NM: How important was silence?

IS: Sometimes we found moments of silence, of supreme, genuine silence. Unfortunately, I am mostly rather restless and talkative. In Jerusalem and in Paris we talked like crazy, told story after story. When he became silent, he was mainly ill-tempered, angry. For no reason in particular. It came suddenly, clear out of the blue.

NM: A darkness.

IS: One can call it darkness, but he would suddenly become angry because I'd spoiled something, said something wrong, behaved badly. For example, the first night in Paris. All at once he was enraged, stopped speaking, kept silent a long time. Later on it came to light that I had been distracted by the surroundings and had looked off in another direction while he was talking to me.

NM: You knew him very well, even when he was still very young. Do you believe that he found his subject, his all important subject, suffering, through the Holocaust, with the Holocaust—that he had been waiting for a great, sorrowful subject, and that subject came to him through Fate?

IS: I thought I knew him well. Paul was really quite contemplative from childhood on and always bore a certain sadness within himself. At the same time he was capricious and could quite suddenly become merry and high-spirited. He sensed his great nervous collapse coming on, but he had always had sorrow within himself, before it came to us. From youth onward, for him it was an existential problem. When his parents were deported, he was in despair, had terrible feelings of guilt. It was very difficult for him to speak about it; he felt alone.

NM: Melancholic?

IS: Yes, depressed. He also spoke of suicide.

NM: Already at that time?

IS: Yes, he spoke of suicide. When my sister committed suicide, again and again we spoke about death and the need to say farewell. He said only a little about his parents, nevertheless the burden was always present.

NM: Then I ask myself, whether these themes, such deep and important ones—suffering, death, annihilation—were not already obsessive themes, reiterated and becoming stronger for his soul and mind, at that bleak "right" moment of horror, in the right phase of his writing.

IS: That's difficult to say—it's also a perilous notion. I don't like to hear people say that Celan is "the poet of the Holocaust," because I don't believe it. He is *also* that. The word is there, although he never pronounces it, quite consciously. Because for him there is no word for it. Judaism is there; Jesus is there; Love is there; the Cosmos is there. All and Nothing. He is called the Jew, the Poet, the One Who Got Away [*der Davongekommene*]. But he did not get away. He could not escape. He carried what is historic and what is Judaic within himself, as I said earlier. From youth onward, for him it was both personal and existential experience. His writing was his life—experience and writing were ONE for him.

NM: Do you think if you had succeeded in getting to Paris two or three days before his suicide that it would have been possible to save him?

IS: Perhaps for that moment it would have been possible.

NM: Where did you get that feeling, where does it come from?

IS: It was his last letter. I also spoke with him on the telephone; and then after the final letter I tried to call him again, but there was no answer. When I was about to leave Paris, in a previous visit he wrote down the address of one of his close friends, and he said to me in Yiddish, "*Ojf nischt zu bedarfn* [Even if useless/even if not to be used]. Surely you know how things are with me." While friends were looking for him, his cleaning lady knew that "une Madame d'Israel" would arrive. Thus he knew intuitively that I would come. When I arrived, I met Gisèle [Celan's wife] at his friend's place. Paul's name in Hebrew was "Pessach." It was just on Passover Evening that Paul disappeared. When Paul once told me quite mysteriously that his Jewish name was "Pessach," he added: "Sounds too Jewish, doesn't it!" We laughed.

NM: You said that the relationship—though it was always important and deep—became even more important after his death. For you and for your husband. And that it took on additional significance.

IS: Yes, the relationship expanded, deepened, and new aspects and perspectives came into play. Concerning my husband, he had a great deal of understanding for me and for what happened to me and to us, but in the end he had his limits.

NM: It gets to a point. And then comes the explosion.

IS: The explosion came, and it was difficult. We had a great deal of tolerance for each other, but there was also ambivalence and conflicts that were difficult to endure. We had to spend some time living apart.

NM: A long time?

IS: A few years. For awhile I lived alone with my daughter.

NM: And your daughter, how did she cope with this?

IS: She, too, had a lot of understanding, but which subliminally made things difficult for both of us. Back then—she was between fifteen and seventeen—it was only natural. My daughter and my grandchildren are also tolerant now. For example, I asked them, too, for their opinion about the publication of the correspondence. They told me that my doubts were exaggerated and that publication is important. Of course I should publish the book.

NM: I suspect there is also a great deal of love for her mother.

IS: My daughter? Perhaps, but she loved and admired her father without reservation. With me, she has had many more conversations; we have spent more time together. Nevertheless, we often had mother-daughter conflicts. So, it was not easy, at the time. Michaela did a lot of crazy things back then. She was in Gymnasium and should have taken her graduation exam, but she did not want to learn.

NM: So, was she, too, in a particular period of her life?

IS: Yes, even my daughter and my husband had their difficulties and were rather complicated, quite separately from me. My husband was not easy to comprehend. He appeared to be balanced, dependable, extremely courteous, earnest and successful, and this was not entirely the case. It wasn't really that he pretended, he just made the impression. He had a lot of charm, and everyone liked him, people held him in high esteem. In our circle of friends my relationship with Celan was really taken very badly.

NM: Yes, it was a time of great tension, but what do you think today about the mythology surrounding Celan? A mythology always arises around an artist. A mythology that exaggerates or alters [its subject].

IS: Or places an official stamp on it.

NM: In what way have you felt this?

IS: Celan basically was and remained a spoiled little mama's boy from

Czernowitz—this I believe only a few knew and saw through.

NM: Yes, you said that to me. A typical one?

IS: Typical. After all, one of the many such children. (I am not now alluding, of course, to his also truly unspeakable gifts.) But in Czernowitz, there was something of a cult of genius. Every second or third child was a genius from whom infinitely much was expected. You, yourself, as well as the others, those less gifted, had to suffer this. And what was genius? That was not so precisely defined. A little talent in figure skating or playing the piano, the ability to speak many languages, especially to "parlez français," study abroad. In Jewish families, this was the case most everywhere. But parents in Czernowitz were insatiable. They wanted the best and meant well; yet in many cases nothing good came of it.

NM: I asked you about the mythology, the image that posterity has made of him. I don't much like it when a great production is made of it all, with the mythology of posterity, posterity as theater.

IS: Yes, there is something like the posthumous history of the great minds, of the artists, etc. There's an afterlife, a kind of iconography, which can become part of each one's fictitious biography. For that very reason, in the case of Celan, I long had to contemplate, to read and reread him again and again, to search and try to pare away the rind to get to what seems true.

The many images of Celan: Celan the dark, stooped man of sorrows . . . Celan, poet of the Shoah . . . Celan the deranged man. . . the sick man . . . the mystic . . . the master . . . the womanizer . . . the counterfeiter and plagiarist . . . the poseur . . . the empty man, the silenced man . . . and yet, and yet, and yet . . . Celan, a genuine poet.

NM: But let's return to his sensitivity as a child.

IS: There was much talk of his bad father who lacked understanding— and of his loving, giving, angelic, and admiring mother. Like most children, Paul received thrashings. Other children simply dealt with them as a matter of course. Paul was more hurt, because he was more sensitive. But what exactly was the nature of his sensitivity? Later the problems Celan had with his father were compared to those Kafka had with his—also a myth. Celan's genius, if one may call it that, was a gift of the gods, and thus the heaviest burden. He felt no one understood him. It could be no other way. He did not endure the loneliness that must have arisen out of this. And besides, perhaps his case is similar to that of Kafka and Benjamin—more and more research always being done at universities and more connections being drawn between them.

NM: Step by step it becomes an academic subject.

IS: But it concerns something else. It must, in their case, be something completely different from an academic debate.

NM: That's why I so enjoy your writing, too, because it is authentic. Sometimes it's also sarcastic and ironic, and I like that very much. Even for the mythology of the Holocaust. Because a great, a huge distortion ensues.

IS: These festivals, these fake Holocaust festivals, evading the subject of memory as a career!

NM: It becomes a ritual, and it becomes theater, almost.

IS: Were it a real, an authentic ritual, which had grown out of experience, it could be valuable, but as it has been handled it is something else. It is business, politics as usual, manipulated by vested interests.

NM: There are so many repetitions, so many rehearsals, until finally the performance is completely artificial, the original notion meaningless.

IS: One becomes blunted, indifferent. Whether and how Celan gets falsified is an open question. What is the significance of Jewishness in his poetry? Was it the *"Anders-sein"* ["otherness"]? Was it the quotation from Tsvetaeva, "All poets are Jews"? On the one hand he was occupied with Levinas; on the other hand, the dispute with Heidegger was very important. This is already difficult to accept.

NM: The Heidegger affair?

IS: Yes, another affair, which disturbed him, about which we also spoke often. Celan was under the spell of Heidegger's language —of *Being and Time*, of concepts like *"Geworfen-Sein"* ["being thrown"]. In the end, Celan felt wounded by Heidegger, although the latter took great interest in Celan.

NM: He was a wholly great authority.

IS: I heard a lot of contradictory information about their final meeting in March 1970 in Freiburg—what Celan wrote to me and what Professor Baumann reports about this encounter. Celan wrote to me that Heidegger did not understand him. Baumann says the opposite: Heidegger listened with complete attention and afterward even recited a something by heart. Heidegger had seen Celan out as far as the gate, then he returned to his other guests and said, "Celan is very, very sick." According to Baumann.

NM: Yes, this is strange.

IS: Celan's so-called "illness" and his stays in French psychiatric care were very bad. Treatment was conventional—not sophisticated.

NM: And today?

IS: About the present time I do not know. But in his time, when he told me about it, it sounded terrible. Of course there were also very good psychiatrists in Paris, but he did not get to them. Nor did he want to.

NM: I'm convinced he did not want to. Did he have this "inner" need for Jerusalem, the "center" missing from his life, in his life as a poet? As an imagined center for his feeling and thinking, not necessary for living in it? An inner, symbolical location, a poetical, lyrical stimulus? Was he experiencing a spiritual need to return to Jerusalem? You told me that he had the notion that you were the daughter of Zion.

IS: That was a bit of an exaggeration. We also laughed about it!

NM: Exactly, but for him, Jerusalem became, so to speak, a metaphorical necessity—dreamy, a lost and absent destination?

IS: A dream of "Heavenly Jerusalem," but also the opposite. There are, among others, two poems about Jerusalem. In one of them, Jerusalem is in the light, *"Das Leuchten"* [The Shining]—that rides toward us: the radiance that approaches "from temples' depths." Then, in the counter-poem, Jerusalem, *"Tochtergeschwulst einer Blendung im All"* [daughter metastasis of a glare in space], Jerusalem is a cancer. He wrote those two poems on one and the same day, "The Shining" and "Daughter metastasis of a glare in space." Two oppositional imaginings of Jerusalem.

NM: You also mentioned provincialism.

IS: Israel is provincial.

NM: Even if international conferences with many people take place, in the end there is still provincialism; they end with highly provincial rhetoric. And here is the split between us and the others.

IS: There is also the opposite. We have very many talented writers in Israel.

NM: And with a vision that is much broader and, one can say, universal. There is now a generation of artists and authors who are more at home in the world, not only here.

IS: The world can be provincial, too.

NM: The world is becoming a small village.

I read the little book about your family and upbringing. I find it interesting that you were in this affluent environment, and that as a child and even later, you never found it easy to endure. You were and you remained, I am convinced, far more authentic and on the left.

IS: Whatever that means.

NM: What this means today we no longer know. But what it meant at that time, we do know, and I ask myself whether, when the Russians arrived—you suffered through that, did you not?

IS: Principally that affected my parents. In the beginning, I did not sufficiently suffer with them in the same way, as I was a very young girl back then.

NM: Your parents and also you, for there was a connection. One cannot deny this. Did one then suddenly understand, things are not as one dreamed, things are different?

IS: About Stalin one already knew beforehand what the reality looked like. But the whole extent of the danger was not clear to us. With the Germans, it happened in a very similar way. My father, for example, took the German occupation better than the Soviet, even though we were in greater danger. During the time of the Soviet occupation, many Jews denounced one another, slandered one another, wanting to protect themselves at other people's expense. There was little loyalty among Jews. My father suffered greatly because of that.

NM: Was there no loyalty then?

IS: Among us, there is often a poor show of loyalty.

NM: And the Jewish Communists—

IS: —were also in jeopardy. Even more than the non-communists.

NM: Were there many?

IS: Comparatively. There were the young, and a whole crowd of drawing-room Communists. On the other side there were the Zionists, the Yiddishists, the Bundists, and others—businessmen and academics, who considered themselves citizens of the world and wanted to go to the West, to America. Celan, for example, as a fourteen- or fifteen-year-old was very active as a Communist. He, too, contributed writing to their illegal newspaper. But long before the invasion of the Russians, he recognized Stalin and withdrew from active participation in Communism. He stuck by his friends from that time, however, and later, too, he wrote and sent letters on to them in the "East." When the Soviets moved in, I remember meeting him on the street. I asked him, "Now what do you think?"

"Now I'm an Anarchist," he replied.

This was already dangerous. At the university, too, he had represented himself as "anarchistic." He kept to his leftist stance. At the time of the student uprisings in Paris he got up on the barricades. Once, late in the evening, he got hungry. He asked a comrade if he thought he would be able to find an open restaurant. "What are you thinking about? We are in the middle of a revolution! *Et tu ne pense qu'a bouffer!*" Then Paul thought, now it's time for him to make his retreat.

NM: And here in Israel you were more or less on the left, no? Rather suddenly.

IS: Yes, but I was not really active—I never belonged to a party.

NM: No, not actively. But in your thoughts?

IS: In my thoughts . . . for example, I'm thinking of the Eichmann trial and the incomprehension of the majority of Israelis, who thought only in black and white, who could never show any understanding whatsoever for Hannah Arendt's attitude. The petition of Buber, [Samuel Hugo] Bergman, and a few other intellectuals moved me in particular, also of my good friend the painter Yehuda Bacon. Do you know of him?

NM: No.

IS: Today he is an Israeli painter; he comes from Prague. As a child he was in Theresienstadt and Auschwitz and lost his family, survived and came to Israel at roughly eighteen years of age. Buber and Bergmann took care of him; he found a home with Bergman, and he got support for his study of painting at Bezalel. Yehuda was a witness at the Eichmann trial. As a youth, he carried the dead out of the gas chambers, that was his job. He survived Auschwitz, and now along with Buber, Bergman and other intellectuals, he signed the petition against the death sentence that would hang Eichmann.

NM: Ah, I did not know this. Really?

IS: Yes, the government and the media swept it under the rug.

NM: Why was that?

IS: It's clear. I believe that in Bergman's diaries one could find a more precise account.

NM: How did you follow the trial?

IS: I am ashamed to confess that I did not closely follow the trial. For me, I believe it was already, as always, hard to deal with what one calls Shoah among us—yet neither would I know how to deal with it any better.

NM: Yes, I understand this very well. I too.

IS: On the other hand I cannot—and I do not—want to forget, either. But I cannot hate. I cannot hate the Germans. I experience and understand all of what happened, in a broad context, not as the responsibility of *one* person or *one* people. I want to learn to comprehend, if one can actually speak of comprehension. But I have no feelings of hatred. Neither do I feel myself to be a victim, although in a certain sense I was—the yellow star, displaced, disenfranchised, and humiliated. I have the feeling of not having suffered equivalent pain; no hunger, no freezing cold, no torments in a camp. This [sense of] survival at-the-edge is excruciating and persists.

NM: And your relationship to the German language? Surely it is far deeper and more important than the one you have to Hebrew?

IS: It's different. Unfortunately, I never immersed myself in the Hebrew language. When I first came here, the Ulpan did not exist, and I had to study privately. When I was in the seminar on music education and later, in my advanced studies, of course I spoke Hebrew and wrote in Hebrew, but it was rather functional, in connection with of my studies. I learned a great deal from my husband, who spoke Hebrew exceptionally well.

NM: How come?

IS: He arrived in the country at the age of thirteen, and he had a gift for learning languages.

NM: From Switzerland?

IS: From Turkey, from Istanbul.

NM: From Istanbul?

IS: He was born in Istanbul and went to a German school. But his parents spoke no German. His father came from Ukraine and his mother's family from Bessarabia. They wanted to emigrate to America. Hermann, my future husband, was the only one in the family who went to the German school and spoke German. He loved both the language and the school very much. He absorbed German from kindergarten on. He told me how he had played his role as a little dwarf in Snow White and the Seven Dwarves. He still knew it by heart. He was a superior student and won prizes—I still own an edition of the Grimms' *Fairy Tales* from that time. He brought his entire German library to Palestine. With his pocket money he bought more antiquarian books in German. He translated Karl May and [Theodor] Storm into Hebrew, for example, "The City on the Sea." For him, Tel Aviv was the city on the sea. So, at thirteen he was already a German romantic.

NM: How was the relationship with the Romanians? Did you have one?

IS: Scarcely at all, on my part. I went to private schools, where there were no Romanian girls. My father had Romanian friends. He also had a Romanian partner in the factory.

NM: No contact whatsoever?

IS: Very little. Except for with the maid.

NM: And how did the Romanians act then?

IS: Then, during the war? I can recall Romanian officers who helped us without asking anything in return. Readiness to help. . . ?

NM: This was in '41, right?

IS: From '40-'41 till '44, we knew a Romanian officer, who by chance, when we had to move into the ghetto, would travel to Arad, where one of my mother's aunts lived. My mother had the idea of filling a big wardrobe-trunk with objects she was fond of, giving it to him, and asking him to take it along with him. We could not take things along with us in any case, naturally. She packed up all the following: books and letters and pictures and silver and cutlery and small objects of art. I still have a few things from there with me in my home today. For example, the silver sugar bowl my mother brought as part of her dowry from Vienna. Also this little mosaic frame. These two pictures our architect painted of our factory, the entrance to the factory. They come from the early thirties. I also have letters from my grandmother to my mother, in gothic script, and many extremely old photographs.

NM: And the officer took it along with him?

IS: My mother managed to pack it all into a gigantic wardrobe-trunk, as marvelously as she could. I can still remember that none of the porcelain broke on the long journey. It was sent with good luck, and the Romanian officer delivered it honestly and loyally.

NM: And he demanded nothing at all in return?

IS: Nothing.

NM: That is extraordinary.

IS: Our aunt sent the wardrobe-trunk from Arad to Palestine after the war (circa 1946). It arrived with all its contents.

NM: Is there anything important about Celan, do you think, that has been neglected? For example, arriving in Paris at the right time?

IS: I don't believe it would have changed anything very much had I arrived in Paris at the right time, which of course I hoped to do. No, I don't believe I could have helped him. I believe that his circle, his environment in Paris, was not good for him.

NM: Would it be possible to be together with him for a long while?

IS: No. That was clear to us. We spoke and wrote to each other about that.

NM: This was felt?

IS: He knew, too, that he was "in the long run unbearable," which he also writes. To speak frankly, I am not one of those women who, as the saying goes, can live only for a man. I can be very present, and I can give a lot, too—but I was afraid of not being able to withdraw and simply be there for the other. This pains me greatly concerning Paul; he required it. That I always wanted more—although I assured him of the opposite—more and more letters and attention, this was, I fear, too much of a burden.

NM: Did he take it? This he needed, too?

IS: I know it was childish, that I would have to acquiesce more and not always expect more from him than he could give.

NM: Really?

IS: I needed attention which, at the time, I also received in large part when we were together. He was very attentive, capable of listening and perceiving and understanding in ways one seldom experiences. He really wanted to know, understand, and recognize.

NM: Who is this woman, who is she?

IS: Yes, he wanted really to know and to see. He could also remember everything imaginable from Czernowitz. Once he asked me if my mother was still so childish. He recalled my mother and every possible situation in our house. And it was true, my mother was somewhat childish. A very dear, sweet mother, but also childish and self-centered.

NM: And his relationship to his son? Was there a real connection, or not?

IS: Paul had a mental image of an ideal family. He wanted this in life. It did not work. He asked too much.

NM: Idealistic . . . a sacred image?

IS: A divine image. Later, though, he had real sorrows concerning his son.

NM: The family there was Catholic, but what was he? Jewish?

IS: Eric is neither a Jew nor a Christian. He has no interest in a tradition of any kind. He loves the circus and learned magic and juggling in a circus school.

NM: And how do you remember Gisèle?

IS: When people were searching for Celan in Paris after his suicide, we met at Lutrand's, one of Paul's friends. She did not want to leave me alone in a hotel and invited me to stay with her. We talked the whole night through. It was a good, open conversation, and we drank whisky, which made many things easier. Gisèle was educated in a convent school, but her rebellion against home came principally through her decision to live with Paul. In my opinion, she admired him greatly, but she was also fearful of him. I believe it was difficult for her to accept and to understand his complex personality. She was very magnanimous, very delicate, one could say aristocratic. Paul also accepted this in her. She was prepared to become a Jewess, to go to Israel. She was prepared to do a lot for him, but he did not want this at all. Worlds lay between the two of them.

NM: Everything for him.

IS: But she was a good artist, and Paul enjoyed giving names to her abstract pictures.

NM: How did Gisèle handle his relationships with other women? His affairs?

IS: This question has already been discussed so thoroughly, that I would prefer to refrain from speaking about it. The one thing I have to add is that I did not experience Celan as a typical ladies' man or skirt-chaser. He sought to have genuine relationships and gave a great deal in a relationship.

—Translated from the German by Rika Lesser

Needing and Being Needed

An Introduction to the Letters of Celan & Shmueli

by   Norman Manea

Ilana Shmueli and I spoke a lot and were silent a lot. I recalled that after a long walk through Paris with a totally silent Celan the great Polish poet Zbygniew Herbert declared that it was the very best dialogue he ever had with anybody. My own dialogue and silence with Ilana Shmueli focused, of course, on Paul Celan and our Romanian, German, Jewish Bukovina, the joy and cruelties of our biographies. (Our conversation is the interview that begins on page 165 of this volume.)

I first came across Ilana Shmueli's name, some years ago, in her letter to Celan that was translated from the German into Romanian in *Lettre Internationale*, one of the best literary magazine in Romania. I was instantly taken by her tone and style, her judgment and sensitivity, which means by her being. "A literary beast," a wonderful and rare one, I told myself. I started to hunt her texts as if I were searching for Milena's lost letters to Kafka.

It came to pass in December 2009, when I was at a conference in Jerusalem, I had, finally, the privilege of meeting Ilana Shmueli, the close friend, interlocutor, and kindred soul of Paul Celan. I immediately recognized in her the embodiment of a Bukovina spirituality and charm, the imprint of a civilized and stimulating environment that once hosted a vivid dialogue between cultures. I recognized the melancholy and frenzy of a time past. We talked about food and dialects, about school and ethnic diversity, about political utopias and dreams of genius, about her great Romanian violin teacher and her faithfulness to the German language, about the Bukovina friends she is still meeting in Israel and around the world. In her small, elegant apartment I recalled the always proper houses of my acquaintances; on the shelves of her walls I saw dear and familiar titles of my old and new readings.

On receiving the literary prize of the city of Bremen, Paul Celan emphasized that he came from a landscape "inhabited by people and books." He meant our cosmopolitan Bukovina, the province in Northeastern Romania where Romanians, Jews, Germans, Poles, Ukrainians, Armenians and other minorities lived together in a vivid and vibrating spiritual atmosphere. This is the region where my family and I lived before and after the Second World War, with a pause of four years, during the war, when we were deported by the Romanian authorities to the concentration camps of Transnistria, a nightmarish place I use to call "Trans-tristia."

This nightmare became the dark subject of many Jewish Bukovina writers and is not missing from my own work. It is also an obsessive topic of

Paul Celan's poetry, the most brilliant and bleak work on "the black milk" of suffering, on the lasting wound of memory. What enhances the lyrical power of his writing is the non-transitive language, the coded and often fragmentary phrasing of his solitude, framing and fermenting the inner life of his own posterity and his powerful, even if fractured and whispered, lament. It is a not a "free delivery" of poetry, because it is heavily paid for by the author himself and all his fraternal addressees. It is poetry of a turbulent silence searching for words as a means of searching for a listener, a fraternal and shadowy YOU, the virtual and unknown interlocutor able to bring to life the lasting ashes of the bloody past and the ever ruined present, in an ultimate and persistent attempt to give life and expression to the ghost of that nightmare. His poetry, despite its locked in messages and its singular, lowered voice, is also an appeal to resilience and revival, without which life and art aren't possible.

In this blurred but still vibrating image of another time and another world we may regain, if only partially, the unavoidably partial and coded remains of the former landscape of people and books called Bukovina, the landscape of our souls in that time and place.

Ilana Shmueli represents, I think, the late but most awaited and desired YOU for the poet. "I am almost sure that we had to travel all the long and difficult roads in order to be ourselves the way we now do—can do—will do?" she writes. The female partner who can be lover, friend, sister, and "so much more," that "you, you with your head shaved," a Bukovina mate, with a common childhood and cultural formation and the shaved head of a survivor, she brought him, after many years of separation, their youthful past but also Jerusalem, the virtual, most dreamt of and unattainable homeland ("Say that Jerusalem is/ as if we, without us, could be we").

Ilana Shmueli is among the most beloved and close addressees of his letters and poems, too.

It is not by chance that writers of the same family of solitaries (Kafka, Beckett) wrote a huge number of letters. Such letters are not the usual, trivial "conversation" and quotidian petty correspondence that Proust so much practiced and despised, as a social, frivolous tribute and mask, unrelated to the artist found in his creative work. In his famous text *Against Saint-Beuve*, Proust speaks about the critic's "inability to understand the originality of genius and the nullity of conversation." Conversation, here, meant the empty appearance of the writer, outside his creative cell, the mundane movement within the social environment, the "external features of a writer's biography and character," not the intimate communication with a friend or lover through letters or even, at another level and code, through a poetic message sent out into the unknown.

We find, in his letters to Ilana—as in his poetry—the "pneumatic" Celan, in his last years of creativity and life, when he so painfully struggled with deep depression and frailty. The difference Celan saw between the inner core of his feelings and their cheap exposure in worldly "conversation" and appearances is visible in his relationship to Ilana and his letters to her, as it is in the difference between his necessarily encoded poetry and the more "usual" poetry of his contemporary poets, who lived lives of more usual comedies and tragedies, and usual nightmares. What he considered the fundamental difference between "thematic" and breathing in his Jewishness, his literary Jewishness, as he wrote to his publisher, Schocken, is related to his most profound, inner self, to his deepest intimacy. Reporting to Ilana on his love, writing, longing for Jerusalem— the three main topics of this important and revelatory correspondence—he speaks of her as his Jewish "double," or rather half of himself.

These letters are written during Celan's last years before his suicide. The very last one is dated April 12, 1970, a week before he disappeared in the Seine. They mark the weight and the intense, melancholy light this intimate binding brought to both of them.

"Needing and being needed is the most elementary and perhaps most essential and beautiful thing that can happen to a person, if one is finally ready for it," writes Ilana. She certainly was ready. "The absurd joy of living. . . was almost foreign to me as a real experience," she confesses. It is a belated and reviving re-encounter with a dear friend, with memories of youth, too, and an awakened dream in the fight for happiness, seen as whatever form love-admiration-tension-trust-devotion take in the completeness of a real couple. "Sometimes I imagine how it would be if I could be young and beautiful for you—with this youthful beauty, strength, immediacy, assurance," she writes, adding, strangely, "which I believe I never had." (Quite an odd statement for anybody who has seen her photos as a young woman.) And yet she knows well, as always, where she stands: "I know what value these things I belong to and the rootedness have for you." She tells Paul: "it is already wonderful no longer to have the obligation to be young," and tries to reassure him, before a most desired meeting in Paris, about their chance "in spite of everything"—age, distance, wounds of the past, marriages (Paul writes in a poem: "As I wear the ring shadow,/ you wear the ring"). Ilana proves always to be wonderfully attentive, even when she is unavoidably needy. "I need a sign . . . / give it to me . . . it is not easy for me to say this." She is affectionate, attentive, wary, generous, understanding, acute, loving. "I love you very much, don't be afraid of it." She is protective ("forget everything complaining in whatever I write to you"), eager to offer and receive, to share and assume responsibilities, to "resolve something fundamental and essential in your suffering," stimulating hope and strength ("for after all, you love it, life—otherwise it couldn't become so torturous for you"). In a remarkable postscript, Ilana tells us in this book that after Celan's suicide, she and his wife, the artist Gisèle Celan-Lestrange, and son met cordially and that Gisèle gave Ilana a letter addressed to her that Celan never mailed.

What about him?

"The powers I had in Jerusalem" Paul writes, referring to their first meeting after his only visit to Israel, "have disappeared." Yet he still sees some progress: "a year ago I was behind asylum bars and thought it would be forever." How is it "functioning in disaster" in a wonderful city that "pushes him down and empties him out," where the streets "nourish" his "mad visions"? Despite the daily unbearable burden to stay alive, despite his loneliness or perhaps because of it ("in the company of highly intellectual people, I could hardly utter a word"), their relationship intensified his daily fight to go on, his tenacious commitment to his poetry. He longs for her ("I translate you over to me"), shortly before his death he is still aspiring to share with her the Kafka dream ("To lift the world into the pure, the unchanging, the true"), and he keeps writing his poems to the very end ("I am struggling . . . I am standing"), as he still keeps Israel between them and with them ("my anxiety about Israel—there I am still myself. As I write you—when you speak, when you write, when . . . I am thankful to you for everything you tell me about Israel, including its dark sides, I am happy that you see it with open eyes—for it is only in this way that can one really love it"). Their love ("that you call it by its name: thank you for that, love, thank you and thank you," he writes her), a love with open eyes for both of them, is enlightening, encouraging, enslaving, a gift and a burden, full of joy and bitterness, and hope and longing and precious, priceless intensity.

The two correspondents are exiles ("going from void to void I would like to be in the right place" writes Paul), he in the unbearable City of Light, which becomes one of bleakness ("hellish emptiness"), she in a land that is devouring its children ("The so dubious Jewish Heimat, from which, however, flight is no more possible," writes the Israeli Ilana, deeply committed to and deeply unsettled by her new homeland). They are essential exiles, everywhere and always, exiles in life and in the world. "Heimat is exile and exile—homeland" is the statement that would be lived by both and signed by them.

And between them are letters. ("There is something very cruel about it, this writing of letters, these little controlled insights," she writes.) In the post office in Jerusalem and Paris they replay, in their own way, the story of *The Little Prince* by Saint Exupéry, obeying the rite of taming each other through much awaited encounters; there they are the correspondents who have written encounters and are more and more dependent on them, never having enough of them, the habit and ritual becoming the center of daily expectations, as could have happened to the Little Prince and his dear fox in their enchanting meetings.

Ilana tells him about her daily pilgrimage to the post office, often saddened and worried by the empty box. Paul has his own stories about his adventures at the Parisian post office. "I always mail the letters at the post office in the Rue d'Ulm, since they are airmail letters they are weighed when they are franked, the official at the counter—the officials plural —know me, they have not failed to take note of the fact that I write to Israel. There are two of them. One is polite, the other, by no means a young man, a few days ago, as I was mailing a journal to Germany as printed matter, opened the package, I saw that for the first time in twenty years in Paris, I would have to be able to describe the facial expression, it spoke volumes, and the hand movements, there I stood like someone who is not trusted.—All right, this exists after all, a little harassment, right, this kind of thing happens.—And today, when I posted the letter to you, it was the same official, and he read the destination, the country of destination, on the envelope, he darted a look at me the likes of which I know from my youth in Czernowitz: he examined me, searched my face for Jewish traits, found them, and attacked me with his hatred, only with his eyes, obviously . . . Why this story, Ilana? But why this question?—You know what it is about, even without this unspoken tiny incident. Yes, you are . . . an outsider, as I am an outsider."

It is a telling story, as is the one told by Kafka about his encounter with a group of Austrian gentlemen at lunch in a spa, when they start to be suspicious about his "accent" and inquire persistently about his origin. Such fragments go beyond their own narrative into a deeper question, essential for our understanding of these great writers, their love affairs, their letters and, in a more general way, not only theirs.

But that's not quite that. In reading Celan, it is good to know that, in 1775, the Austrian Emperor was taken by the grandeur of the Tara de Sus (Upper Country), then part of the Moldavian Principality, and decided to incorporate it into his empire. In 1777, the population of the newly acquired Austrian province swore an oath of allegiance to Vienna, an occasion that was celebrated with great pomp and ceremony in Czernowitz. The Romanian Prince Grigore Ghica, a fierce opponent of the acquisition, was assassinated on the very day of the celebration.

Bukovina was to be named a Grafschaft, or duchy, like the Austrian Tirol. The name *Bukovina* derives from the famous beeches of the Upper Country, Latin name *silvae faginales*, *buk* in Slavonic, *bucovine* in the old Romanian chronicles. The Germans called it *Buchenland* (the land of beech trees), translated in Romanian as *tara fagilor*. Bukovina was recognized as an autonomous Habsburg province, had its own Parliament—Dieta—with a Romanian president and with a quite diverse and democratic representation of minorities, Romanians, Jews, Poles and Ukrainians, not a very common situation at that time. It also had representatives in the central parliament in Vienna.

After the First World War, in 1918, Bukovina was reincorporated into Great Romania. During the Second World War, the Northern part of it was occupied by the Soviet Union. So the name of the capital changed in two centuries from the Romanian Cernauti to the Austrian Czernowitz and finally to the Ukrainian Chernivtsi. It tells the strange destiny of this troubled and mesmerizing region, a region described as a mixture of a great forestry, German village, a Polish-Ukrainian ghetto, a Viennese-style metropolis, a profoundly Russian fragment and, believe it or not, a modern American model.

The former province of Bukovina is currently divided between its Ukrainian Northern part, with the capital in Chernivtsi, and the Romanian Southern part, with the capital in Suceava, the former royal residence of Stephan the Great, the glorious Moldavian king, the place of my birth and my childhood.

During my visit in 2003 to the former Czernowitz, called little Vienna, now known as Chernivtsi, I had to discover the heavy Slavic (or rather Soviet) imprint on a quite shabby city.

Bukovina means not only a beautiful landscape but also a seductive cultural hybrid of great originality and richness. The extraordinary Romanian monasteries, UNESCO art monuments, with their exterior frescos more than five hundred years old, the Jewish old cemetery of Siret, also a UNESCO monument and aesthetically more impressive than the Old Jewish cemetery in Prague, are only a small historical remembrance of this heritage, to which we should add such great names as the Romanian national poet Mihai Eminescu; Jewish poet Itzik Manger; Abraham Goldfaden, the creator of the Yiddish theater; the German writer Gregor von Rezzori; the Hebrew writers Aharon Appelfeld and Dan Pagis; the German-Jewish poets Paul Celan, Rosa Ausländer, and many, many others. It's not by chance that the region was considered the "placenta of Romanian Literature," and Czernowitz meant for many not only "Jerusalem on the Prut" or a kind of "second Jewish Canaan," the "Jewish Eldorado of Austria," but also—in the words of Zbygniew Herbert—"the last European Alexandria."

If we mention these brand, holy beautiful names of the area, we may also want to add Traian Popovici, the Christian major of Czernowitz in the dark Nazi time, who tried with admirable tenacity to halt the deportation of the Jewish population, to defend it from the anti-Semitic policy of the Antonescu regime and the persistent anti-Semitism of the Romanian nationalists of the region. When his efforts failed, he wrote about the camps in Transnistria with a deeply felt empathy and pain: "From across the millennia, a tragic destiny has united the Babylonian captivity with the inferno of starvation, disease, and death in Transnistria . . . The looting at the assembly points along the Dniester River of whatever personal possessions the deportees still had, the long marches, barefoot, in wind, rain, sleet, and mud, the hunger and thirst, could be from the pages of Dante's *Inferno*." (Except the *Inferno* was and is a supremely great work of the imagination, and the camps were absolutely real—Dante a privilege to remember, and the camps painfully necessary to remember, still part of the lives of the remaining survivors and their companions of the human race, likely and unlikely.)

Surely, this correspondence gives us a more intimate understanding of Celan than we have without it. Further, the correspondence introduces Shmueli, an important writer, to English readers for the first time. Ironically, the correspondence is a living account of their old and new environment, their art, culture and intelligence, their extraordinary dialogue. We also encounter the "people and books" that inhabited their biography and their writing, the history of their inner landscape. It is a gift that deserves the deepest and consistent attention—that "natural prayer of the soul," as Ilana Shmueli says, quoting Celan and Malebranche.

N. M.
Bard College
August 2010